SOCIAL MEDIA MUSINGS

Book 2

GEORGE WAAS

authorHOUSE®

AuthorHouse™
1663 Liberty Drive
Bloomington, IN 47403
www.authorhouse.com
Phone: 833-262-8899

Published by AuthorHouse 07/05/2022

ISBN: 978-1-6655-6401-4 (sc)
ISBN: 978-1-6655-6400-7 (e)

Print information available on the last page.

This book is printed on acid-free paper.

CONTENTS

INTRODUCTION

Earlier this year, I wrote a book titled "Social Media Musings." In the introduction, I said I am the product of two professions driven by inquiry and skepticism, journalism, and law.

I noted that both professions are founded upon logic, rational thinking, critical analysis, and sound judgment. So, when I see something that doesn't make sense, defies logic, is irrational, or otherwise off-the-wall, I ask questions and search for answers.

I also confessed that I am a Facebook junkie, although not necessarily enamored with social media. There is certainly far too much misinformation, flat-out wrong information, etc., being spread on social media. And we know that "a lie travels around the globe while the truth is putting on its shoes."

In my earlier book, I said that, for the most part, I kept my opinions to myself, or shared them with family and friends, until the January 6, 2021, attack on our nation's capital. Since then, taking to heart the note on the Facebook page that says, "What's on your mind," I've posted my thoughts and opinions about various situations on a variety of subjects. Many of my posts are quite lengthy, solely because of the importance I place on fact, analysis, reason, logic, critical thinking, and sound judgment.

I then included in my book, in chronological order from January 6, 2021, to February 2022, my posts on a variety of subjects, mostly—but certainly not all— on politics. Since that book was published in March 2022, I continued to post of Facebook, hoping to continue a national dialog on issues of great public importance.

Here is Book 2 of my social media musings on Facebook.

WELL, THAT DIDN'T TAKE LONG

Well, it certainly didn't take long for the Republicans to bash Supreme Court nominee Judge Ketanji Brown Jackson as a "pawn of the radical left." I suppose to the Republicans, anyone who is sensitive to civil rights, voting rights, academic freedom, history, science and just about any issue that involves rational thinking, critical analysis, sound and reasoned judgment, etc., would be considered a radical by today's Republican Party standards. After all, this is the party that believes that the January 6 attack on the Capitol was "legitimate political discourse;" supports Trump's Big Lie of a non-existent "rigged election" despite all evidence to the contrary; supports wild and crazy conspiracy theories, etc. etc., etc., ad infinitum ad nauseam. And, of course, these same folks would have us believe Justice Amy Coney Barrett is not a pawn of the radical right wing. If it weren't a serious matter, these Republican bashers would be a great cast for a comedy show, a real laughingstock. Only those few Republicans who still have some spine and won't genuflect to the party's Mar-A-Lago menace are to be taken seriously.

FURTHER PROOF THAT THE MEANING OF THE U.S. CONSTITUTION DEPENDS ON THE RULE OF FIVE

As a majority of the Supreme Court appears poised to strike a dagger into Roe v. Wade and just about end the federally recognized right to an abortion, it is important to remember this vital truism once again. The Constitution means whatever a majority of the justices say it means. With nine justices on the Court, the "rule of law" is determined by a majority, or five. Whether a vote on a particular case is 5-4, 6-3, 7-2, 8-1 or 9-0, at the end of the day, it only takes five.

The first ten amendments to the Constitution are called the Bill of Rights. These rights are deemed fundamental, which means they are given the highest order of protection and preference.

The cases are legion that every word in the Constitution is important and must be given due consideration. This of course applies to the amendments; and with regard to those amendments, even their order must be considered. Yet, all rights conferred by those amendments are fundamental.

Now, for the proof of my rule of five statement.

The Second Amendment deals with the right to bear arms. It provides that "A well-regulated Militia, being necessary to the security of a free State, the right of the people to keep and bear Arms, shall not be infringed."

Note the order of the words. It certainly appears that the primary direction of this amendment is toward the first few words; that is "A well-regulated Militia…."

Until relatively recently, this amendment was considered a collective right; that is, one that applied to a recognized group, regulated by law, the purpose of which is to provide the necessary security of a free people through the state. But then, the Supreme Court changed this view by declaring that the right to bear arms is an individual right for one's personal protection.

So, how did the Court manage to separate the first clause regarding a legally organized and regulated military unit, from the second clause which deals with the right of the people? By simply separating them and treating them differently.

In District of Columbia v. Heller (2008), the Court said the Second Amendment is naturally divided into two parts: its prefatory clause (A well-regulated Militia, being necessary to the security of a free State) and its operative clause (the right of the people to keep and bear Arms shall not be infringed). In other words, what the Court did was to differentiate between a collective right separate from an individual right. The purpose of the first, or prefatory, clause was to protect the states in their authority to maintain formal, organized militia units. Under the second and separate operative clause, individuals would be protected in the ownership, possession, and transportation of firearms.

Thus, by placing the primacy of the amendment on the second clause over the first, the Court, by 5-4, created an independent individual right to bear arms. Why did they choose the second clause over the first, or why didn't they consider the amendment as a single entity, with the first clause modifying the second? Because five justices decided to separate them by way of a parsing of words and phrases. Simple, isn't it?

But now we have the Ninth Amendment. That amendment provides "The enumeration in the Constitution, of certain rights, shall not be construed to deny or disparage others retained by the people." Again, we are dealing with a fundamental right.

This amendment says the rights set out in the Constitution, including amendments, are not to be interpreted to deny or treat as unimportant other rights retained by the people. Thus, logic compels us to conclude that there are other rights not set out in the Constitution that are nevertheless recognized by it. To put it another way, the rights of the people are not limited to those set out in the Constitution.

So, what might they be? The Court has recognized that the Ninth Amendment guarantees the right to vote, travel and a right of privacy. And the right to an abortion. These rights can be argued as fundamental because they flow from the Ninth Amendment's recognition of their existence vested in the people at its adoption.

If the Court, again by a majority, decides that the right to an abortion is no longer protected, then the question naturally arises what other rights "retained by the people" can be similarly denied or disparaged?

All it takes is five justices who are quite capable of parsing words and phrases to bring about their chosen conclusion.

By the end of its current session, the Florida Legislature will have passed Gov. Ron DeSantis's pet bills banning the teaching of Critical Race Theory, a "Don't Say Gay" bill and an anti-WOKE bill. These bills are at the heart of a culture war being waged between the right and left wings of the political spectrum.

The debate over these bills has been heated, with bitter accusations exchanged between and among legislators. And we know this is part of a broader culture war being waged in other predominantly Republican-led states.

Central to these debates is what precisely this legislation means in actual practice. Opponents say it will stultify education, chill the teaching of history and other classes, wreck academic freedom, permit discriminatory behavior, etc. Supporters say none of these concerns is well-founded, and that all of the subjects can be taught, but without making students feel guilty. These laws allow those offended to sue those who violate the law.

Here's the obvious problem with these laws. What offends one person may be perfectly acceptable to another. And while it appears CRT isn't taught in Florida schools, someone might believe it is, while others might not. Is this difference of opinion on what is actually being taught going to be the basis of a lawsuit?

There is a legal doctrine, however, that defenders of these laws are going to have to overcome, and that is called the void for vagueness doctrine. It is based on our constitutional law.

Briefly put, a law is void for vagueness and unenforceable if it is too vague for the average citizen to understand. It is premised on the notion that a constitutionally protected interest can't tolerate permissible activity to be chilled if it can't clearly be understood what exactly is prohibited. This doctrine applies to penal statutes with criminal or quasi-criminal civil penalties, and civil statutes where the interest invaded by the vague law is a constitutional right requiring a strict scrutiny standard of inquiry, such as free speech. These three bills noted above fit into this free speech/strict scrutiny category.

There are several reasons a statute may be considered vague; in general, a statute might be void for vagueness when an average citizen cannot generally determine what persons are regulated, what conduct is prohibited, or what punishment may be imposed. For example, criminal laws that don't state explicitly and definitely what conduct is punishable are void for vagueness. A statute is also void for vagueness if a legislature's delegation of authority to judges and/or administrators is so extensive that it would lead to arbitrary prosecutions. Related to the "void for vagueness" concept is the "unconstitutional vagueness" concept. A law can be "void for vagueness" if it imposes on First Amendment freedom of speech, assembly, or religion. Again, this is where these, and related laws, fit.

It seems reasonable to conclude that if the legislators themselves can't agree on what is and is not permissible under these soon-to-be-adopted laws, how can we expect the citizenry and the judges who will consider challenges to agree on what these laws forbid, and what is allowed?

Stay tuned.

WHY IS JOURNALISM DECLINING? PART I

My initial reaction to the 60 Minutes segment is what is the projected model for the profession over the next 10 years? Are there enough journalism students coming out of the colleges to support the profession? Or is the declining number of newspapers symptomatic of something else, such as the rise of social media, the proliferation of TV news outlets? After seeing Dana's comment, I have similar concerns. I had understood that the number of law students graduating each year is increasing, so why would the number of firms be contracting? What else is happening that would drive a contraction of firms while simultaneously producing greater numbers?

Ben's comment also raises an interesting point. Having worked at two newspapers in the 60s, I can attest to political bias back then, only it was far more subtle, such as placement of articles in the paper, the amount of space given to particular articles, etc. One of the things that bothers me about the Democrat is the lack of an editorial stand. Both newspapers I worked for each had a strong community presence in part because it had a strong editorial stand. Those papers were the consciences of their respective communities because, knowing that the editors were watching, public officials actually feared a negative editorial. How does a newspaper rise to the level of being the conscience of the community if it has no voice on the editorial page? How does a newspaper keep "them" honest if it can't point out misfeasance or malfeasance in its editorial comment? I am certainly not suggesting that the news should be biased, but a newspaper should have a voice through its editorial page. In fact, usually the items most read were the comics and the editorial page. Relying on individual columns from community members isn't enough. They speak for one person; on the editorial page, the newspaper strives to speak as a powerful, organized and respected force of conscience to the community it serves.

WHY IS JOURNALISM DECLINING? PART II

Having a background in the disciplines you mention certainly makes a person well-rounded, and with an inquiring mind and a strong work ethic, would make outstanding reporters. Having a degree in journalism certainly doesn't take the place of those with the qualities you mention, but the implication of your comments may be reflective of a more serious concern: the lack of that strong work ethic and inquiring mind necessary to be a successful reporter. Life is too much a search for instant gratification, a what-can-you-do-for-me-now attitude. Working 9 to 5 may be far more appealing than taking a job where one can spend days or weeks chasing down leads and gathering facts by digging, digging, digging.

Perhaps I'm overgeneralizing, but this attitude may play a role. Plus, those with the broad backgrounds you suggest have other professions and occupations awaiting them, which probably pay better. So, there's the competitive edge consideration as well. Taking both into account may well explain at least part of the reasons for the decline in newspapers. On the matter of content, perhaps the newspaper think pieces are going the way of the Dodo bird. Maybe those in-depth articles are great for the Atlantic or other magazines, but not for the daily newspaper. Again, there's that attitude of wanting information quickly and easily; don't bother me with something that takes time to read. Back when we started (and you stuck with it; I didn't), journalism was considered literature in a hurry. Not so anymore. Newspapers are to be read quickly over breakfast or on the run, not digested. Give the reader the basic facts and move on. If more is wanted, go online and see if a magazine or a newspaper dedicated to more in-depth stories has a more detailed version of that hard news article. As Jack Webb of Dragnet fame would say "Just the facts, ma'am."

CENTRALIZING OF POWER

The current conservative makeup of the Court indicates strongly that it will curb the EPA's ability to deal with greenhouse gases. Conservatives are strongly pro-business, and just about anything that imposes burdens on business is frowned upon by the conservative core. They also oppose what they call the administrative state, under which, according to them, an agency, given broad rulemaking power by Congress, assumes for itself the power to legislate. Essentially, it is up to Congress to spell out exactly what range an agency has in adopting rules. However, the reality is Congress can't possibly address every potential risk, condition, nuance, etc., of events in legislation. Therefore, in the past, Congress would set general guidelines, but leave the details to the experts; those in the agency who have the knowledge, training and experience to deal with the particular problem.

Since the Republicans gained control of Congress–and state legislatures–they have been rolling back this administrative state, opting for greater control of the executive branch by presumably providing more detailed (however that may be crafted) descriptions of agency powers and duties. In the past as well, courts would defer to agency expertise, taking the view that they, not the courts, have the knowledge, etc., that courts simply don't have. That, too, has been eroded by the Republican Party. Now, courts can second-guess agencies on their rulemaking authority, looking to the legislation for the agencies' authority and deciding what is and is not within the agencies' purview in adopting rules. I might add that the Republican Party (at least in Florida) has curbed local government's ability to adopt ordinances under home rule. You can see how they have successfully assumed greater control over the executive branch and local governments. This is the party that professes a belief that government shouldn't be centralized–unless of course they are in power to centralize.

FOR BILL BARR, IT'S TOO LITTLE AND TOO LATE

Former Trump Attorney General Bill Barr has a memoir coming out next week entitled "One Damn Thing After Another." In his book, Barr blasts his ex-boss, saying he has "shown he has neither the temperament nor persuasive powers to provide the kind of positive leadership that is needed" and that the Republican party should move on from him. Barr also rejects Trump's Big Lie" that he was cheated out of re-election by a "rigged" election. He further writes that his former boss could have won the 2020 election if he had "just exercised a modicum of self-restraint, moderating even a little of his pettiness," according to the Wall Street Journal.

Trump no doubt will put Barr's missive in the same category as the previous dozen or so books that are critical of him and his administration, calling it a hoax, part of a witch hunt, and full of lies. Of course, Trump has neither filed a defamation lawsuit against any author, nor has he ever testified under oath about any matter covered by any of these books. No doubt this pattern will continue with this latest swipe at the former president. And we all know why. Well, except perhaps his True Believers who swear by every word he says as being the gospel truth.

What is ironic about Barr's book is that this is the same man vouched for Trump, was the ex-president's hatchet man, was in the street with him during the demonstration that led to the famous picture-taking in front of a church with bible in hand, weaponized the Department of Justice to suit Trump's wishes, etc., etc.

We know why Barr turned the tables on his former boss. Had this book been about the virtues of Donald Trump, his incredible leadership skills, his calm demeanor in times of crisis, his exemplary persuasive forensic skills, etc., etc., etc., the book would have been advertised as humor-fiction. Plus, sales of such a book wouldn't have covered either the advance or publishing costs.

So, Barr decided to come clean now, so that his book will do the same thing that the other Trump exposes have done: make lots of money.

But for Barr, there is no gold star for dissing on Trump. And there is no glory that will get him in the good graces of those who lambasted him for dereliction of duty during his years as the nation's chief law enforcement officer.

No doubt others who served Trump will come clean as well; not so much to set the record straight, but to sell books.

The time to set the record straight was years ago. But Barr chose to remain silent so he could keep his highly visible, cushy job. Then, after the curtain came down, he was suddenly struck by a wave of conscience; hence, his cathartic endeavor.

I'm certainly not taken by his mea culpa; I will not buy his book. Neither will I buy any book written by a former staffer who, either stood idly or did Trump's bidding while in office, now has a change of heart and wants to set the record straight. To sell books, of course.

For Barr—and for them—it's a matter of too little and too late.

WHAT DOES THE REPUBLICAN PARTY REALLY STAND FOR?

In answering this question (assuming Republicans really want to answer), please don't bore us by reciting the platitudes and generalities such as limited government, less taxes, more freedom, liberty, justice, blah, blah, blah. God, motherhood, and apple pie are also non-responsive. These words are full of sound and fury but signify nothing unless backed up with action. And by action, I don't mean the usual laundry list of things Democratic you don't like, which is just about everything they support.

Pray tell, let us know what precisely it is that you actively support. List those programs that are you seeking to carve into law. Set out the positive aspects of your programmatic agenda. Other than tax breaks for the super-wealthy and stacking the courts with far-right wing conservatives, what else do you favor?

Since Republicans are passing so many bills in the various states, and so many are hoping to stop Congressional investigations of Trump and his acolytes, allow me to pose these questions to see if we can get a definitive answer to this question.

To my Republican friends and those out there who support the party, do you believe:

- Donald Trump was defeated by a "rigged election?"
- The January 6, 2021, Capitol event was "legitimate political discourse?"
- The history of racism, anti-Semitism, and other examples of prejudice against groups on the basis of race, ethnicity, or gender, should be taught, warts and all, in our schools and colleges?
- That local home rule is whatever the state, through its legislature and governor, says it is; therefore, the state should decide what ordinances local governments can and cannot pass?

- Vladimir Putin is a strong leader, and the United States should have leadership that emulates Putin?
- That there are some "nice" anti-Semitics and White Supremacists in our country who are making positive contributions to society?

I think these points represent a good place to start actually finding out what the Republican Party stands for.

It does seem, however, that there are currently two factions in the party: the Trumpites and the rest. Hopefully, the answers to the general question posed at the beginning, and the six listed points, will be a unified one. But whatever answers we get will be far better than hiding behind glittering generalities. The pablum or Kool-Aid may work for some, but certainly not the rest.

GOVERNOR FAVORS WHITE NATIONALISTS OVER DEMOCRATS

Arizona Republican Gov. Doug Ducey says he favors supporting White Nationalists over Democrats. According to Merriam-Webster's Dictionary, White Nationalist is one of a group of militant white people who espouse white supremacy and advocate enforced racial segregation. White supremacy is defined as the belief that the white race is inherently superior to other races and that white people should have control over people of other races. They support Neo-Nazism and Fascism.

I don't know whether he said this out of ignorance or if he really means it. But what he is saying is that he prefers those who support anti-Semitism and racial segregation—and the hatred that drives both–over candidates for a political party that has been in existence since 1828, with roots going back to 1792, and that has produced 16 presidents.

Can you imagine the outrage if a Democratic governor said he supported a despot or tyrant who killed his own people like Josef Stalin or Pol Pot over a Republican candidate? Why they would be foaming at the mouth venting the most vicious bile at a Democrat who dared to compare these despicable lowlifes with a member of the cherished Republican Party–the party of freedom, liberty, justice, law and order, unity, blah, blah, blah.

Yet, where is the outrage over this governor's scandalous and despicable remark? Does the Republican Party endorse or support this kind of comment? Is this to be tolerated as we near the 250th anniversary of the birth of our country?

Have they no decency? Have they no shame?

OBSERVATIONS AND INSIGHTS ABOUT THE ROLE AND IMPORTANCE OF A FREE PRESS

At a time when certain members of a certain political party, whose actions are called out and exposed by the media, lambast the press as "the enemy of the people," it's important to recall what some of our great leaders thought about the importance of a free and independent press. Here are some quotes compiled by Michael Josephson.

- Were it left to me to decide whether we should have a government without newspapers, or newspapers without a government, I should not hesitate a moment to prefer the latter. Thomas Jefferson
- Nothing can now be believed which is seen in a newspaper. Truth itself becomes suspicious by being put into that polluted vehicle. Thomas Jefferson
- Our liberty depends on the freedom of the press, and that cannot be limited without being lost. Thomas Jefferson
- No government ought to be without censors; and where the press is not free no one ever will. Thomas Jefferson
- I am… for freedom of the press, and against all violations of the Constitution to silence by force and not by reason the complaints or criticisms, just or unjust, of our citizens against the conduct of their agents. Thomas Jefferson
- Where the press is free and every man able to read, all is safe. Thomas Jefferson
- No experiment can be more interesting than that we are now trying, and which we trust will end in establishing the fact, that man may be governed by reason and truth. Our first object should therefore be, to leave open to him all the avenues to truth. The most effectual hitherto found, is the freedom of the press. It is, therefore, the first shut up by those

who fear the investigation of their actions. Thomas Jefferson

- Considering the great importance to the public liberty of the freedom of the press, and the difficulty of submitting it to very precise rules, the laws have thought it less mischievous to give greater scope to its freedom than to the restraint of it. Thomas Jefferson
- By a declaration of rights, I mean one which shall stipulate freedom of religion, freedom of the press, freedom of commerce against monopolies, trial by juries in all cases, no suspensions of the habeas corpus, no standing armies. These are fetters against doing evil which no honest government should decline. Thomas Jefferson
- It astonishes me to find… [that so many] of our countrymen… should be contented to live under a system which leaves to their governors the power of taking from them the trial by jury in civil cases, freedom of religion, freedom of the press, freedom of commerce, the habeas corpus laws, and of yoking them with a standing army. This is a degeneracy in the principles of liberty… which I [would not have expected for at least] four centuries. Thomas Jefferson
- The Constitution of most of our states (and of the United States) assert that all power is inherent in the people; that they may exercise it by themselves; that it is their right and duty to be at all times armed and that they are entitled to freedom of person, freedom

of religion, freedom of property, and freedom of press. Thomas Jefferson

- Whoever would overthrow the liberty of a nation must begin by subduing the freeness of speech. Benjamin Franklin
- Congress shall make no law respecting an establishment of religion or prohibiting the free exercise thereof. James Madison
- Knowledge will forever govern ignorance; and a people who mean to be their own governors must arm themselves with the power which knowledge gives. James Madison
- The freedom of the press should be inviolate. John Quincy Adams
- As unbalanced parties of every description can never tolerate a free inquiry of any kind, when employed against themselves, the license, and even the most temperate freedom of the press, soon excite resentment and revenge. -John Adams
- "When the public's right to know is threatened, and when the rights of free speech and free press are at risk, all of the other liberties we hold dear are endangered." – Christopher Dodd
- "Freedom of the Press, if it means anything at all, means the freedom to criticize and oppose." – George Orwell
- "Our liberty depends on the freedom of the press, and that cannot be limited without being lost." – Thomas Jefferson

- "Freedom of conscience, of education, of speech, of assembly are among the very fundamentals of democracy and all of them would be nullified should freedom of the press ever be successfully challenged." – FDR
- Freedom of expression – in particular, freedom of the press – guarantees popular participation in the decisions and actions of government, and popular participation is the essence of our democracy. – Corazon Aquino
- "The liberty of the press is essential to the security of the state." – John Adams
- "The people must know before they can act, and there is no educator to compare with the press." – Ida B. Wells
- "A free press can be good or bad, but, most certainly, without freedom a press will never be anything but bad." – Albert Camus

---

SERENA WILLIAMS SAYS SHE SHOULD HAVE WON 30 OR 32 CHAMPIONSHIPS. BUT SHE DIDN'T

No doubt about greatness. However, saying she let them get away diminishes her opponents, who beat her fair and square on the tennis court–the only place where it counts. Maybe she didn't bring her best game when she lost; but that's not her opponents' fault. Maybe they didn't bring their best games when Serena beat them. After all, they could make the same claim because there's no way to disprove it. The easiest thing to do is talk about how you're better than those who beat you. Boxers do that all the time when they lose. How many times have you heard a winner say he/she should have lost? Doesn't happen.

Maybe she feels she should have won, but the fact is she didn't. Her record speaks for itself; her greatness as a tennis player is assured. She doesn't need to go this route. Indeed, no great athlete needs to shudda, cudda, wudda the past. It doesn't make them any better.

Q: WHY DO LIBERALS AND PROGRESSIVES ALWAYS WANT CONSERVATIVES TO DO THE DIFFICULT STUFF?

A: Probably because all conservatives do is blast away at Democratic programs and actions. Where is the right-wing plan to deal with real problems for real people? The Democrats have historically given us social security, Medicare and Medicaid, and on and on. What program have the conservatives and regressives given us that have benefitted the most? You're for less government–unless a woman wants to control her own body, or a kid wants to wear a mask. You're for law and order–but it was the far-right wing that attacked police officers on January 6 at the Capitol, egged on by a former president who's the right wing's solution to all problems. You're for less taxes–but have no problem giving huge tax breaks to the wealthy.

Let me ask you a question: Do you agree that Putin is smart and savvy? Is this your example of Republicans stepping up? Do you agree that Trump lost a "rigged" election? What exactly does the Republican Party stand for? Marjorie Taylor Greene and her ilk? I'm certainly not saying the Democrats have all the answers; they've been far too timid and tepid in some of their responses and have made their share of missteps. But the current version of the Republican Party offers no solutions, except to attack the foundations of our Democracy. But perhaps you believe that what happened on January 6 was nothing more than "legitimate political discourse."

REPUBLICANS WARN DOJ ANY PROSECUTION OF TRUMP WILL LEAD TO POLITICAL WAR

This is a blatant attempt at political extortion. In so many words, the Republicans are saying Trump should be exempt from prosecution for all crimes he committed upon threat of turning the filing of charges into a political war, since they believe most people think politics is involved anyway. As payback, the former GOP might block appointments, Biden's legislative agenda, etc. But they're doing that anyway. The DOJ could be intimidated by this, simply declare that the law will drive the decision to prosecute, or fight fire with fire. Biden is used to some level of political in-fighting. He could back channel a counter-threat: pass an acceptable version of his entire legislative program and Trump is off the DOJ hook. Remember, Biden has three more years to play with. He could give the Republicans a deadline to pass his agenda with some bipartisan support. In any event, the administration shouldn't stand idly by in the face of this threat. Everything at this level is politics; but the overriding question must be whether crimes were committed. Remember, no one–no one–is above the law.

LOCAL OFFICIALS' PUBLIC GET-TOGETHER QUESTIONED

Let's see now. It's all a matter of coincidence that these four local public officials just happened to be on the same flight going to the same place at the same time. And, of course, public officials are entitled to have a private life and engage in purely social activities, so long as public business isn't discussed. And whether they did or did not is purely a matter for the honor system. So, these officials didn't discuss public business–scout's honor. But what about how this appears to the public? Doesn't appearance count? Mustn't public officials not only avoid impropriety, but even the appearance of impropriety? Naturally, they are making out Porter to be a troublemaker who had the audacity to question their integrity and honesty. But Porter didn't create the situation; these officials did. And whether they like it or not, when they are elected or appointed to high public office, they have voluntarily chosen to live in a goldfish bowl, where everything done in public is under a microscope. The public has the right to know the who, what, when, where, why and how of this eyebrow-raising get-together, such as where were they going, and who paid for the airline tickets. Porter asked legitimate questions that deserve an answer rather than an accusation and brushoff. History teaches that when the questioner is accused, the accusers are usually hiding something.

THE GREATEST THREAT TO DEMOCRACY

Recently, Arizona's Republican Governor Doug Ducey said he would rather vote for a candidate who attended a White Nationalist rally because a Democrat is far worse. This was echoed by former Attorney General Bill Barr who, after lambasting his former boss for lying about his election loss and threatening democracy, nevertheless said he would vote for Donald Trump in 2024 "Because I believe that the greatest threat to the country is the progressive agenda being pushed by the Democratic Party, it's inconceivable to me that I wouldn't vote for the Republican nominee."

If you read nothing else in Heather Cox Richardson's article today, read what is quoted below.

"This same conviction that Democrats must be stopped at all costs is pushing the drive to destroy democracy by concentrating political power in state legislatures. In a dissent this week, four right-wing Supreme Court justices indicated they support a further step in that concentration, backing a legal argument that state legislatures have ultimate power to determine their own voting procedures, including the selection of presidential electors, regardless of what a majority of voters want.

Under the dressing of new legal terminology, this is, at heart, the old state's rights argument. If a state's legislature can determine who gets to vote, a minority can control that legislature and entrench itself in power, passing laws that keep the majority subservient to those in control. It was this very concept Congress overrode in 1868 with the Fourteenth Amendment to the Constitution, saying that no state could deprive a citizen of the equal protection of the laws.

Resurrecting it now would pave the way for a January 6th–type coup through the law, rather than through the plots of a ragtag mess of insurrectionists."

All the currently dominant right wing Republican Party needs to do is, through enough state legislatures, decide that no what the actual, truthful vote tally is, the Republican candidate gets the major 270 electoral college votes, and the party takes over the executive branch of government. With a like-minded Congress, the former GOP controls the legislative and executive branches of the federal government. With favorable interpretation of the laws by an increasing right-wing judiciary and the Republican Party has a fait accompli; precisely what Richardson sets out in her eye-opening column.

The Republican Party's campaign to portray the Democratic Party as the epitome of evil, the true "enemy of the people," is under way. The party leadership is unabashed about their true motives, with efforts under way to whip up the frenzy and anger of enough voters in key states to buy into this. How Americans deal with this existential threat to our almost 250-year-old experiment will foretell our future.

MOST OF JUDGE KATANJI BROWN JACKSON'S RULINGS HAVE BEEN REVERSED ON APPEAL

To make any kind of cogent analysis, you must consider the amount of time a judge serves on the bench and the type of cases that generally arrive at the particular court. So, for the point you make, you might want to compare the amount of time–and volume of cases–of recent appointees, such as Justices Gorsuch, Kavanaugh and Barrett. Then, look at how many times these three judges were reversed weighed against the amount of time they served as judges whose decisions were subject to review by higher courts. Then consider the types of cases that generally come before each court. For example, you might well find different types of cases before a federal court in New York than one that sits in Montana. A circuit court that covers New York and New England areas might have different types of cases than one that covers midwestern states.

In short, there are a host of factors that must be considered rather than merely counting case numbers. And finally, consider the volume of cases each judge handled. Some judges simply work faster than others; this is no different than the general workforce; people work at different paces. So, if a judge writes 100 opinions and is reversed four times, while another judge writes 20 opinions and is reversed three times, certainly the first judge has been reversed the most; but that judge also has a better record because he/she has handled more cases successfully. And yes, to help you in conducted a real analysis, all three justices had decisions reversed before arriving at the Supreme Court. Judge Jackson has served as a federal judge about as long as both Gorsuch and Kavanaugh; Barrett served about three years. Experience counts, as does one's real track record, taking all relevant factors into account.

AUTHORITARIANISM V. FREEDOM. HISTORY DOESN'T LIE

History teaches how authoritarians behave, particularly when pressured. The game plan is obvious. First, they begin their ascent by promising all sorts of goodies through platitudes of freedom, liberty, justice, law and order, etc., and going after "them," the anointed "enemy of the people." And that's fine with those who agree with this part of the playbook. But eventually, authoritarians are questioned, and when this happens, they will turn on their own supporters to keep everyone in line and on the same page. What Putin is doing is no different from what other dictators have done when the rising number of doubters begin to ask questions.

Here, by no stretch of the imagination, when you have some Republican Party leaders endorsing supporters of White Nationalism over Democrats, while other party leaders remain silent, you should have a good idea where the Republicans want to take the country. Around the world, Democracy is imperiled because it's more complex, difficult to maintain and preserve than it is to simply obey an authoritarian, at least for a while. But the yearning to be free burns in the human spirit and is part of our nature. Eventually, supporters of the oppressors become oppressed. And so it goes.

HOW TO WRITE A BOOK

The hardest part about writing a book is getting started. Each one of us has had different life experiences. We each have different, unique stories to tell, opinions to exchange, ideas to share, etc. In my five published books, I tried to follow each of these points. The key is to write something you know something about. I made a commitment to write by first sitting down and writing an outline of what I wanted to say. I spent a few days working on that outline. Each outline was no longer than a couple of pages. Then, when I sat at my computer, I found it amazing at how each point of the outline seemed to flow from my fingers on the keyboard to the page on my screen.

At times, I was writing 1000 or more words day! My books range from about 25,000 to 125,000 words each. At 1000 words a day, you can see how long it took for me to write my books. This, of course, demonstrates the second hardest part of writing–sticking to it after getting started. But once you start writing, the information will flow, and you will look forward to each day as another day closer to doing something very few do–write a published book.

FOR REPUBLICANS, IT'S BUSINESS, AS USUAL

The Republican-controlled Florida Legislature can pass laws to intimidate voters through an election police force; impinge on academic freedom by controlling what can and can't be taught about race, gender, and ethnicity; allow businesses to sue local governments; etc., etc., etc., ad nauseam, yet they refuse to pass a law to help people living in genuine fear of their condominiums. How dare for them to impose safety requirements on condominium developers! There is nothing new here, of course. For the Republicans, it's really about business, as usual. Safety doesn't matter; culture "correctness" does.

ARTICLE IN THE ATLANTIC: THE RED STATE ONSLAUGHT STARTS WITH FLORIDA

Remember, the definition of "woke" is, according to the Merriam-Webster dictionary, "actively attentive to important facts and issues (especially issues of racial and social justice)." Therefore, being anti-woke means being against active attentiveness to important facts and issues;

in other words, being ignorant or indifferent. To those who consider being "woke" evil, and are content to being anti-woke, are they happy being ignorant or indifferent? That is a question only they can answer.

The point here is to see these laws as set out in this article for what they are: a form of cancel culture directed at historical teachings; an assault on academic freedom; an attack on voting rights from the vantage point of knowing how historically people have voted as groups; elevating large businesses over individual rights and safety; and on and on. All of this is being accomplished in the name of freedom, liberty, rule of law, etc. What is being accomplished in the topsy turvy world of Newspeak is the opposite. Be aware. Be very aware.

WHAT DOES BEING "WOKE" MEAN?

So many people believe that being "anti-woke" is a source of pride, and that being "woke" is some sort of evil. But do the anti-wokers really know what the word means?

The Merriam-Webster Dictionary defines "woke" as being "aware of and actively attentive to important facts and issues (especially issues of racial and social justice)." The dictionary cites this sentence as an example of how this word is used according to its definition: "But we will only succeed if we reject the growing pressure to retreat into cynicism and hopelessness. … We have a moral obligation to "***stay woke***," take a stand and be active; challenging injustices and racism in our communities and fighting hatred and discrimination wherever it rises. — Barbara Lee

A thesaurus containing antonyms, or opposite words, for "woke" list such words as oblivious, neglectful, unthinking, thoughtless, inattentive, unknowing, careless, indifferent, etc.

Logically then, being anti-woke means being unaware of and inattentive to important facts and issues, particularly regarding racial and social justice and hatred and discrimination where it rises.

Further, it means being oblivious, neglectful, unthinking, unthinking, etc., when it comes to important facts and issues regarding social justice and hatred and discrimination regardless of its source.

Knowing what the words "woke" and "anti-woke" mean, why would anyone want to be considered unaware, inattentive, etc.?

IS RUSSIA NO LONGER AN "EVIL EMPIRE" TO THE REPUBLICAN PARTY?

President Ronald Reagan called the Soviet Union–Russia and its puppets–an "evil empire." Even with the last Soviet Union leader, Mikhail Gorbachev, Reagan was most cautious; recall "trust, but verify." No president in modern times has cozied up to a Russian leader, until Donald Trump came along and couldn't do enough to kiss Putin's ring.

After Trump praised Putin and said he believed the Russian dictator when he said he didn't help Trump get elected in 2016–rejecting the findings of his own government investigative agencies, including the FBI–his minions in Congress, and elsewhere, dutifully followed suit.

Now, with Putin finally showing his true colors–those of a tyrant, a despot stubbornly clinging to the past glory of a long-gone empire –and with daily reports of the horrors he is inflicting on the Ukrainians, even the ever-loyal asset Trump has softened his praise, saying Putin "has changed." Of course, Trump has no knowledge of the tried-and-true axiom that a leopard can't change its spots. No, Putin hasn't changed; he's still the same master manipulator who saw a good thing in Trump and used it to his advantage.

What is so stark about the Trump-Putin relationship is how it has transformed the Republican Party. Remember that traditionally the Republican Party has been anti-communism, anti-socialism. In fact, whenever they rail against anything Democrat today, they'll accuse them of being socialist or communist or both–whichever piece of red meat the pliant audience will accept at the time.

But wonder of wonders! Today we have the extreme right wing of the Republican Party still praising Putin and dissing the Ukrainian leadership. One such example of the intellectual level of the party is one Rep. Madison

Cawthorn, who called the Ukrainian president a "thug," no doubt giving some minimal aid and comfort to Putin. But although Cawthorn was condemned by some party leaders, that condemnation certainly did not include all of the party faithful.

But here's the rub. If the Republican Party is so adamant in its opposition to socialism and communism, why does it allow Trump and his cronies to cozy up to the very embodiment of socialism and communism–Vladimir Putin? A fair question is whether it's really the Democrats who are pushing a radical authoritarian, totalitarian agenda. After all, you don't hear any Democrats praising Putin, wanting to leave NATO as Trump does, or calling the Ukrainian president a thug.

And we won't even discuss Trump's praise for China's Xi Jinping or Kim Jong-un of North Korea. Remember, you are judged by the company you keep. "When you lie down with dogs, you'll get up with fleas."

"AMERICA, OUR WARNING LIGHTS ARE BLINKING RED"

This is the headline for a column in Today's USA TODAY and, considering the angry tone of too many social media posts, it is imperative that we take heed of its warning, and act appropriately.

If you follow Facebook, you've seen posts discussing important issues. But as you scroll down the list of posts, you will unfortunately see such comments as "It's all (insert party or place on the political spectrum) BS." Or perhaps "What an idiotic comment." Maybe even an "Only a moron would believe that nonsense." You get the point. Personal attacks that offer no fact, just simple, knee-jerk angry retorts.

Today's column by Pearce Godwin makes a critical point: we can engage in dialogue and disagree mightily, so long as we keep the conversation directed to issues, not personalities. Name-calling certainly raises the level of anger; however, it does nothing to bring people to at least understand where the other side is coming from. Ad hominem attacks are no substitute for marshalling facts and offering opinions based on facts. A personal attack on the writer is more a statement about the attacker than the writer. If a person's response is nothing more than a personal attack, that person usually has no facts to back up his/her opinion, so with nothing else to offer, they go into attack mode.

Calling someone "stupid," "idiot," "moron" might make him/her feel good, but to the wider audience on social media, this kind of attack backfires—unless the attacker in on a website where this name-calling is not only tolerated but accepted as the norm. There are a few of those out there. We know where they are, and most of us simply avoid them.

The rest of us must do our part to make sure conversations aren't taken to the gutter. As adults, we can discuss and debate issues without limitation; indeed, our country was founded on debate and discussion. It was not founded on attempts at demeaning people by resorting to name-calling. What might work for juveniles on the playground (until they get some good parenting) won't work in the adult world. Name-calling must never be an acceptable substitute for facts, logic, common sense and critical thinking.

TRUMP'S "BIG LIE" CONCOCTED BEFORE ELECTION TOOK PLACE

Today, we learn that it was the White House itself that invented the "report" that the election was stolen, even before the election took place, and then used that report to justify the Big Lie that 19 state legislatures have relied on to restrict voting.

Historian Heather Cox Richardson, in her column today, cites this incredible report from The Guardian's Hugo Lowell. This report alleges that Donald Trump's claim that he lost the 2020 election because of Dominion Voting Systems—a report that Trump used to justify his attempt to overturn the election, including a plan to assume emergency powers—was not written by a volunteer lawyer after the election, as previously understood.

In fact, it was written by a senior White House aide, Joanna Miller, who worked for key Trump advisor Peter Navarro. Navarro incorporated the Miller report into one of his own, which he and aides had begun to write two weeks before the election even happened.

I hope this latest bombshell is proven false; but it does further explain why so many White House personnel have fought vigorously to avoid having to testify under oath before Congress.

If the Democrats tried to pull off a stunt like this–conjuring up a deliberately false cover in the event of election loss–the Republicans would have gone ballistic in their rage, seeking criminal punishment and long-term imprisonment for such outrageous, anti-Democratic behavior.

Where is the Republican outrage over this? If this report is true–and so far, there's been nothing offered to counter it–it says a lot about how little those involved care about our institutions.

The extreme right will likely remain silent, perhaps offer a tepid "he shouldn't have done it" response, or more likely dismiss this report as fake news created by the liberal media–the "enemy of the people–blah, blah, blah. Just the same old tired "red meat" refrain when they have nothing else to counter being caught with their hands in the cookie jar.

Meanwhile, as revelations continue to pile up, we can only wonder what the congressional investigative report will look like when it comes out later this year. Calling it a blockbuster will be an understatement.

Of course, it will be dismissed by the usual suspects just as they've dismissed multiple revelations in the past, hoping the voters won't be bothered by the investigative report's contents. They'll just call it more noise trying to deflect from their freedom, liberty, justice, law and order chants.

Democracy requires each of us to be responsible for our conduct, and it is our duty to match their words with their conduct. That's where the rub really is.

WHAT KEY REPUBLICANS PROMISE TO DO: READ BETWEEN THE LINES, AND BE WARNED

Recently, Florida Sen. Rick Scott proposed an 11-point plan he titles "Rescue America." As you read his plan—and I strongly recommend that you do with a critical eye—be aware that Scott has his sights set on the presidency down the road, and with this plan, he's looking to gain the same traction former House Speaker Newt Gingrich did with his Contract for America in 1994. You recall that plan was instrumental in electing a Republican majority to Congress that year.

To be sure, Scott's plan is full of platitudes about freedom, liberty, law and order...you know, the kind of language designed to get the head to nod up and down in agreement, so long as you don't consider that, as with any plan designed to get traction, the devil's in the details.

Here is a list of 12 of the more than two dozen actual policy matters contained in his plan. The quotes are from Scott:

1. The government would never be able to ask you to disclose your race, ethnicity, or skin color "on any government form."
2. The US military would engage in "ZERO diversity training" or "any woke ideological indoctrination that divides our troops."
3. If a college or university uses affirmative action in admissions, it would be "ineligible for federal funding and will lose their tax-exempt status."
4. The wall along the US southern border would be completed and named after former President Donald Trump.
5. All Americans would pay some income tax "to have skin in the game."
6. All federal legislation would have a sunset provision five years after it passes.
7. "No federal program or tax laws will reward people for being unmarried or discriminate against marriage."
8. No government form would offer options related to "gender identity" or "sexual preference"
9. "All social media platforms that censor speech and cancel people will be treated like publishers and subject to legal action."
10. No tax dollars could be used for "diversity training or other woke indoctrination that is hostile to faith."

11. No dues would be paid to the United Nations or "any international organization that undermines the national interests of the USA."
12. "The weather is always changing. We take climate change seriously, but not hysterically. We will not adopt nutty policies that harm our economy or our jobs."

Focus on numbers 5 and 6. "For number 5, currently, about half of Americans don't pay taxes because their taxable income doesn't meet a minimum threshold. It is estimated that Scott's plan will impose taxes on half of the country. Get that, folks. This is a tax hike for millions—from the political party that claims to be for less taxes!

For number 6, this sunset would include Social Security and Medicare, among other social network programs. Read that again. Scott's plan would eliminate these programs that have become part of America since the days of the Great Depression forward. For those Republicans who are receiving, soon will be receiving, or hope to receive these benefits, this should be a red flag for you.

While many Republicans voiced their support for this plan, some did not. One Republican leader said he won't support any plan that raises taxes on half of America and sunsets Social Security and Medicare. That person is Mitch McConnell.

But he's getting on in years; he will soon be replaced. Scott's plan—like Gingrich's—is directed to the future of the Republican Party and its plan for America.

Read the plan in its entirety; ask yourself questions. Be informed. And be warned.

MY LIST OF "100" GREATEST INSTRUMENTALS OF THE ROCK ERA

I am a creature of lists. I want to know the 10 greatest of this; the 100 best of that—you get the idea. I doubt I'm alone in searching lists. I am also a product of the music of the 50s and 60s. I doubt I'm alone here either, although there is an age factor involved in favoring this musical genre.

Recently, I decided to create a playlist on my Alexa that consists of what in my view are the top instrumentals of the rock era. I searched my memory and came up with about 40. Then I went to Google and came up with 99. But I wanted to round it off by including one song not from the rock era, but one I consider the greatest instrumental of the Big Band era. I think you'll be able to figure that one out.

I mentioned what I had done to a friend, who suggested I might want to share it in case others might like to do the same. So, here is my list of what I consider the greatest instrumentals of the rock era—with emphasis on the 1950s through the 1960s–in no particular order. And my one exception. I hope my list brings back memories, and if you decide to create your own playlist, I hope you enjoy your walk down memory lane as much as I do.

1. Autumn Leaves Roger Williams
2. The Lonely Bull Herb Albert
3. Midnight in Moscow Kenny Ball
4. Bumble Boogie B. Bumble
5. Swinging Safari Billy Vaughn
6. Wonderland by Night Bert Kaempfert
7. Poor People of Paris French orchestra
8. Stranger on the Shore Acker Bilk
9. Pipeline Chantays
10. Last Date Floyd Cramer
11. Quiet Village Martin Denny
12. On the Rebound Floyd Cramer
13. Honky Tonk (pts. 1 and Bill Doggett
14. Miles of Bad Road Duane Eddy
15. Petite Fleur Chris Barber
16. Because They're Young Duane Eddy
17. Bongo Rock Preston Epps
18. Theme from "A Summer Place." Percy Faith
19. Cast Your Fate to the Wind Sounds Orchestral
20. The Entertainer Marvin Hamlisch
21. Canadian Sunset Hugo Winterhalter
22. Java Al Hirt
23. Apache Jorden Inman
24. A Walk in the Black Forest Horst Jankowski
25. Red River Rock Johnny and the Hurricanes
26. Forever in Love Kenny G.
27. Songbird Kenny G.

28. Love is Blue Paul Mauriat
29. Soulful Strut Young-Holt Unlimited
30. Music Box Dancer Frank Mills
31. Patricia Perez Prado
32. Yakety Sax Boots Randolph
33. Lisbon Antigua Nelson Riddle
34. The Stripper David Rose
35. Hooked on Classics Royal Philharmonic
36. Sleepwalk Santo and Johnny
37. Wipeout Surfaris
38. Sail Along Silvery Moon Billy Vaughn
39. Hawaii Five-Ventures
40. Walk Don't Run Ventures
41. Washington Square Village Stompers
42. Guitar Boogie Shuffle Viscounts
43. Calcutta Lawrence Welk
44. Classical Gas Mason Williams
45. Rumble Link Wray
46. Let There be Drums Sandy Nelson
47. Teen Beat Sandy Nelson
48. Rise Herb Albert
49. Pink Panther Theme Henry Mancini
50. Fifth of Beethoven Walter Murphy
51. Cherry Pink and Apple
52. Blossom White Perez Prado
53. A Taste of Honey Herb Albert
54. Happy Organ Dave Cortez
55. Alley Cat Bent Fabric
56. Blue Tango Leroy Anderson
57. Spanish Flea Herb Alpert

58. Ghost Riders in the Sky Ramrods
59. Fancy Pants Al Hirt
60. Moonglow Theme from Picnic Morris Stoloff
61. No Matter What Shape… T-Bones
62. Yellow Bird Arthur Lyman
63. Memphis Lonnie Mack
64. Soulfinger Bar-kays
65. Green Onions Booker T and MGs
66. Take Five Dave Brubeck
67. Tequila Champs
68. One Mint Julep Ray Charles
69. Never on Sunday Don Costa
70. Music to Watch Girls By Bob Crewe
71. So Rare Jimmy Dorsey
72. Percolator Twist Billy Joe and the Checkmates
73. Tea for Two Cha Cha Tommy Dorsey
74. Theme from Exodus Ferrante and Teicher
75. St. Elmo's Fire David Foster
76. Raunchy Bill Justis
77. Baby Scratch My Back Slim Harpo
78. Batman Theme Neal Hefti
79. Canadian Sunset Eddie Haywood
80. Asia Minor Kokomo
81. Wade in the Water Ramsey Lewis
82. Maria Elena Los Indios
83. Love's Theme Love Unlimited
84. The Crazy Otto Johnny Maddox
85. Love Theme, Romeo and Juliet Henry Mancini
86. Last Night Mar-Keys
87. Grazing in the Grass Hugh Masekela

88. The Hustle Van McCoy
89. The Sound of Philadelphia MSFB
90. The Good, the Bad, the Ugly Hugo Montenegro
91. Mexico Bob Moore
92. Manhattan Spiritual Reg Owen
93. Only You Frank Pourcel
94. Wild Weekend Rebels
95. Fly Robin Fly Silver Connection
96. Wheels String-a-longs
97. Telstar Tornadoes
98. Chariots of Fire Vangelis
99. Dueling Banjos Eric Weissberg
100. In the Mood Glenn Miller
101. Gonna Fly Now Bill Conti

ATTACKING DESANTIS WON'T BE ENOUGH; THE DEMOCRATS MUST DO BETTER

To those of you who believe as I do that Ron DeSantis should be defeated in November, it's important to be realistic here. DeSantis has galvanized the right wing, and he's very appealing to Republican voters generally. With changes in voting laws–changes targeted at historic demographic voting patterns and practices–it will be extremely difficult for any Democrat to defeat him. You might even chalk it up as a near impossibility unless he makes a major misstep with his ardent supporters. And who knows what that will take.

The real task before the Democrats is the run-up to the next presidential election. Right now, there are several Republican wannabees, such as Texas Gov. Greg Abbott, Texas Sen. Ted Cruz, Missouri Sen. Josh Hawley, and perhaps one or two others, who have visions of presidential sugarplums dancing in their heads. And of course, there's still Donald Trump. The point here is that if Trump falters–and with all the investigations under way, that is a real possibility–each of the others will undoubtedly try to show that he is more of a true conservative than his opponents. Which means more right-wing than his opponents. In short, each one will provide his own version of more red meat for the true believers; each one will try to make the red meat darker and darker.

The Democrats can hope that these perceived frontrunners falter by effectively devouring one another. But that won't be enough. And attacking DeSantis–or Trump or the other wannabees–won't be enough, either. Thus far, the Democrats have been far too timid and far too tepid in challenging the overriding extremism that has permeated the Republican Party. The Democrats must reach out to moderate Republicans and Independents, expanding the tent. They must fully explain what the anger and program opposition by the right wing really means for the future of our nation. Democrats can't forget that Trump, with all of his flaws, came just a few thousand votes in a few key states from being re-elected. And unless the courts intercede, Democrats will have to deal with getting people registered and to the polls in the face of the many changes made to voting laws driven by Trump's Big Lie of a rigged election–a plan he hatched with his cronies before the election so that he could justify his loss. This is the challenge that is before the Democratic Party. And time is growing short.

WHO IS REALLY BEING INDOCTRINATED?

"Indoctrination" is defined as "the process of teaching a person or group to accept a set of beliefs uncritically.'

As you read the following, consider this definition, with emphasis on the last six words.

Recently, much has been said and written about Critical Race Theory. Conservatives believe this is being taught in schools, is a blatant form of indoctrination, and passed laws to ban its teaching. Others chimed in by saying that CRT isn't taught and it's really nothing more than a means of arousing anger over a non-existent matter and chilling academic freedom.

One dictionary source defines CRT as "an academic and legal framework that denotes that systemic racism is part of American society — from education and housing to employment and healthcare. (It) recognizes that racism is more than the result of individual bias and prejudice. It is embedded in laws, policies and institutions that uphold and reproduce racial inequalities."

Central to this is set out in The Color of Law, written by Richard Rothstein, who argues that segregation is not so much driven by individual prejudices, or de facto segregation, but de jure segregation; that is, laws and policies passed beginning in the 1920s by local, state, and federal governments that promoted discriminatory patterns that continue to this day. The author cites residential zoning laws as a primary example.

About 25 states now ban any instruction or teaching that America is inherently racist, as well as any discussions about conscious and unconscious bias, privilege, discrimination, and oppression. These points also extend beyond race to include matters related to gender.

The opposition to CRT is the view that it is a form of indoctrination. This was the rationale used by Florida Gov. Ron DeSantis in promoting his anti-woke legislation: "We won't allow Florida tax dollars to be spent teaching kids to hate our country or to hate each other. We also have a responsibility to ensure that parents have the means to vindicate their rights when it comes to enforcing state standards. Finally, we must protect Florida workers against the hostile work environment that is created when large corporations force their employees to endure CRT-inspired 'training' and **indoctrination**." (Emphasis added.)

When that word is used, the first thing the audience must do is strip out the anger and emotion it evokes and look at the definition. Then, ask this obvious question: who is being asked to accept without question a set of beliefs?

If a theory has a factual foundation, then it's not so much a belief, but an opinion or pronouncement based on fact. If CRT is wholly theoretical, this can be easily demonstrated if there are no facts to support it. But if there are facts that, when woven together, form a non-theoretical conclusion, shouldn't students be made aware of this? After all, isn't education a search for the truth? Doesn't our system of education encourage children to become independent and critical learners, who understand that seeking the truth, no matter how difficult or challenging that truth might be, is a vital component to becoming an informed, aware and active citizen? The answer should be obvious.

Unfortunately, "indoctrination" has been weaponized to make the audience believe that others are trying to manipulate you or your loved ones or friends. It connotes an evil and sinister motive behind the message.

What should also be obvious is that we—all of us–are constantly being bombarded with messages that are designed to indoctrinate.

Think of religious teachings, or product advertising. In these, and no doubt other examples you can think of, we are being asked to accept a certain set of beliefs without inquiry.

The power of religion is immense. If you doubt this, visit the Vatican, Notre Dame Cathedral in Paris and Montreal, Westminster Abbey in London. I could go on and on. I have been to each of these, and others throughout Europe, and saw up close the power of faith. Religions teach a set of morals and dogma. Dogma is defined as "a belief or set of beliefs that is accepted by the members of a group without being questioned or doubted." Does this definition ring a bell?

When you see an ad on TV or in the print media, you asked to accept a set of beliefs about that product, without question.

I hope this shows that indoctrination is not an inherent evil; it all depends on who is doing the indoctrination, who is being indoctrinated, and for what purpose.

THE SENATE SUPREME COURT CONFIRMATION HEARING: THEATER OF THE ABSURD

The scenario is predictable: the far-right Senators will try to make political theater out of the process, in part as payback for the Gorsuch and, more to the point, the Kavanaugh hearings. Those senators will further endear themselves to their supporters and embarrass themselves in the eyes of everyone else. And then Judge Jackson will be confirmed.

Less than a year ago, Republican Sens. Graham, Collins and Murkowski voted to confirm her to the appeals court. Only Murkowski is up for re-election this year. Graham, however, has already labelled her as part of the "radical left"–which is par for the course when you don't believe there is such a thing as the radical right. Also, last time all Democrats voted for her, including both Manchin and Sinema. Still, I don't think even some of the wild-eyed want to have folks believe her race had anything to do with their votes.

It's kind of a double-edged sword for them: she has the highest rating from the ABA, has more judicial experience than Trump's last pick. and a wealth of experience unmatched by several now on the Court. The opposition's only chance is to paint her as radically out of touch–a relatively easy sell with the far right; a laugher for the rest considering that the last three were accused of being out of touch and they managed to make it through the gauntlet of the absurd that has now become these types of Senate hearings.

THE REPUBLICAN PARTY AS RADICAL RIGHTISTS

The Republicans rail against the Democrats just about every day, accusing them of being radical leftists, leading America down the path to Socialism, Communism, etc. What is missing from this predictable diatribe, however, is what precisely do the Republicans mean? Is it Social

Security, Medicare, voting rights, civil rights, abortion, interracial marriage, rebuilding our infrastructure, taxing the super-wealthy so that they pay more taxes than a stock clerk or store manager? What exactly is it that the former GOP is taking issue with that justifies these accusations?

To the contrary, with the latest thanks to Historian and Author Heather Cox Richardson, we know exactly why the current version of the Republican Party has become identified as right-wing extremism.

According to her column today, 70 percent of Americans support same-sex marriage. But not the Republican Party.

She continues: "In 2012—the most recent poll I can find—89% of Americans thought birth control was morally acceptable, and the Centers for Disease Control and Prevention reported that as of 2008, 99% of sexually active American women use birth control in their lifetimes." But not the Republican Party.

"And even the right to abortion, that issue that has burned in American politics since 1972 when President Richard Nixon began to use it to attract Democratic Catholics to the Republican ticket, remains popular. According to a 2021 Pew poll, 59% of Americans believe it should be legal in most or all cases." But not the Republican Party.

Richardson notes that "(a) full decade ago, in April 2012, respected scholars Thomas Mann, of the Brookings Institution, and Norm Ornstein, of the American Enterprise

Institute, crunched the numbers and concluded: 'The GOP has become an insurgent outlier in American politics. It is ideologically extreme; scornful of compromise; unmoved by conventional understanding of facts, evidence, and science; and dismissive of the legitimacy of its political opposition. When one party moves this far from the mainstream, … it makes it nearly impossible for the political system to deal constructively with the country's challenges.'"

And yet, in the last decade, the party has moved even further to the right.

GOODBYE MOO

This was published when we lost our kitten in March 2021. We received a reminder in March 2022 that it had been a year. I was again moved to tears as I re-read this.)

My wife and I had to euthanize our pet kitten Moo last month. We had him just over 2 ½ months. He was 4 ½ months young.

In December 2020, I wrote about how Moo and his sister, Floof, came into our lives and joined our family in November of last year, when they were barely two months old. We never had kittens at such a young age, and we enjoyed how the two of them played together, scampering through the house, jumping from chair to table to counter (driving our two older cats to distraction), curious about their surroundings, getting into everything, and generally doing all things little kittens do. We loved these beautiful little babies. I called Moo my little boy; referred to him often as little one.

Shortly after we brought them home, we took them to our vet for examination and kitty shots. And then we received devastating news that Moo tested positive for feline leukemia. This is a virus that affects the immune system. Prognosis is 3-5 years. The thing about feline leukemia is that it weakens the immune system, making a cat susceptible to all types of illnesses. Cats don't die from the leukemia; it's the ensuing illness.

We vowed that we would give Moo the best life we could, making sure he got the best medical treatment available.

A few weeks later, Moo had an attack. He was gasping for air and threw up. But it passed that day, he resumed kitten antics, and we thought nothing further about it. However, the next day, he had another attack, only this time he ejected mucous. We immediately made an appointment with our vet and took Moo in for examination. As we waited in the parking lot (a COVID requirement), our vet called my cell phone and asked if she could do an x-ray, as perhaps he might have swallowed something. After a few more minutes, a staff member came out and told us the doctor wanted to see us in the clinic.

When we saw the x-ray, we were shocked. A huge baseball-size lymphoma had formed in Moo's chest cavity and was pressing on his esophagus; he was at risk for suffocation.

The doctor said surgery was out; he wouldn't survive that. Chemo and steroids wouldn't reduce the size of the tumor. The vet didn't have to tell us about options; we could see it in her eyes. Doctors won't make that ultimate decision; they must depend on you to reach the only obvious one.

Harriet and I were devastated. We cried like babies. A few hours ago, Moo was an active little kitten. Now, we had but a few precious moments to say our goodbyes. We were overwhelmed. To see our adorable little kitten about to be put down broke our hearts.

Moo had given us so much joy and laughter. He was the ringleader of our four felines. He made our two 10-year-old senior cats, Mandy and Sandy, stare in wonder as he frolicked through our home; and his frequent tussles with his sister Floof delighted us, while giving each other a lifetime playmate. Or so we thought.

Through our sobs and tears, Harriet held Moo in her arms, and I petted him as the vet injected him. Moo let out a yelp and then fell still. After a second injection, which Moo didn't feel, she checked his breathing and said he was gone.

As we have done for our previous three pets that we lost–our dog Pepper and two cats Rudy and Jolly–we had him cremated, ordered a stone for Moo and will bury him next to them. Moo's stone carries this message that is all so true: "pawprints on our hearts."

Losing Moo is different. While Pepper, Rudy and Jolly lived full lives, Moo was with us only 2 ½ months. Our first three pets were ill and at the end of their lives; we had time to say our goodbyes. Moo was active and full of life even on his last day, when we were faced with the grim reality that his genetic line deprived our little one of his life.

But as pets do, Moo taught us something about ourselves. They are God's little creatures who give us unrequited love in return for what is hoped will be loving and caring owners. Studies have shown that pet ownership is good for one's mental and emotional health. They help reduce stress and keep you engaged. They are wonderful companions.

To be sure, not all pet owners treat their animals with love and devotion. And we certainly wish they did. But we do. And while we remember our precious little Moo for the laughter and joy he brought us, we now know all too well the pain of losing such a small, loving pet at such a young age.

We know Moo never had chance; that x-ray told us his life was over. But it doesn't lessen the pain of losing a pet we loved, especially one so young and full of life. He was just a little baby.

When we visited our family in Gainesville on Valentine's Day weekend, our two young grandchildren gave us a framed photo of Moo; it's the one shown below. That photo, in the frame they made especially for us, now sits on our dresser, a constant reminder of our precious little one.

As for Floof, since our older cats live in their own orbits, we will continue to give Moo's sister plenty of love and attention, enjoy her kitten antics, and be particularly attentive to any signs of loneliness, although research shows felines operate by scent, and scents don't last very long. So, Floof will most likely have no memory of her brother for more than a few days or weeks at the most.

Yes, it hurts to lose a pet, and since they don't live as long as we do, losing a pet is part of life. But while they're with us, they teach us about love and devotion, and how fragile life is. There really is no greater lesson.

So, thank you Moo, my little boy, for being a part of our lives. You have left your pawprints on our hearts. We will never forget you little one.

Goodbye Moo.

<1>

HOW DO JUDGES INTERPRET THE CONSTITUTION?

With the Senate hearing on the nomination of Federal Appeals Judge Ketanji Brown Jackson under way, and with so much discussion focused on constitutional interpretation, I think it worthwhile to discuss briefly how judges and justices perform this arduous duty.

Having argued many cases on constitutional law during my more than 40 years of active practice in both federal and state court, including the United States Supreme Court and Florida Supreme Court, I believe I have a certain understanding of how this is accomplished.

At the outset, note that nowhere in the United States Constitution is there any description of how it is to be interpreted. The Court, in Marbury v. Madison (1803) established the principle of judicial review in the United States, meaning that American courts have the power to strike down laws and statutes that violate the Constitution. In the 219 years that have passed since then, the Court hasn't set out how constitutional issues should be decided.

What has developed over the years are two overriding schools of thought on constitutional interpretation. It is admittedly difficult to capture every element of these two interpretive approaches. In the interest of avoiding hyper-technicalities, I offer these thumbnail descriptions to highlight their meanings.

One school is called the originalists, or textualists. This is the method used by conservatives who believe that the words of the Constitution can only mean what the framers intended them to mean when it was adopted. Justice Antonin Scalia was one of the most forceful modern advocates for originalism, a theory that treats the Constitution like a statute, and gives it the meaning that its words were understood to mean at the time of adoption. As a textualist,

Justice Scalia totally rejected reliance on legislative history or legislative intent. As he said in 2008: "It's what did the words mean to the people who ratified the Bill of Rights or who ratified the Constitution." In explaining his theory of interpretation, he said the Constitution is a "dead" document.

This designation is in direct opposition to the second school of thought on constitutional interpretation, living constitutionalism or judicial pragmatism. This concept or theory is relied on by liberals and is based on the notion that the Constitution has relevant meaning beyond the original text and is an evolving and dynamic document that changes over time as societal conditions change over time. In sum, the Constitution as a "living" document requires that the views of contemporaneous society should be considered when interpreting key constitutional phrases.

Predictably, those who favor one theory oppose the other.

Retiring Justice Stephen Breyer has recently criticized the "originalist" approach, calling on judges to focus more on the Constitution's goal of an active, participatory democracy, noting that this approach can be at odds with that goal. Anti-originalists point out that by interpreting the Constitution at the time of its adoption, and its amendments at their time of adoption, some basic rights such as abortion, same-sex marriage, interracial marriage, contraception, privacy, and others associated with the living constitutionalist theory would not exist today. They also contend that interpreting the Constitution in accordance with long outdated views is often unacceptable as a policy matter, and therefore an evolving interpretation is necessary. Another view is that the constitutional framers specifically wrote the Constitution in broad and flexible terms to create such a dynamic, "living" document.

Supporters of originalism argue that the Constitution should be changed through the amendment process, and that the living constitutionalism theory can be used by judges to inject their personal values into constitutional interpretation, thus the label of an "activist" judge who "legislates from the bench."

But consistency has been called the last refuge of the unimaginative, and proponents of both theories have on occasion crossed over to the other side to reach a particular result. At bottom, an activist judge is one who issues an opinion others disagree with. It's a convenient label that is easy to attach and easy to be accepted without thought. Believing that judicial activism is only found in one theory is a myth.

JACKASSERY!

Yesterday, during the Senate confirmation hearing for Judge Ketanji Brown Jackson, Republican Sen. Ben Sasse, after listening to rants from fellow Sens. Ted Cruz and Lindsey Graham–and no doubt including Josh Hawley–expressed concern about cameras in the Supreme Court, but then said "Cameras change human behavior. I think we should recognize that the jackassery we often see around here is partly because of people mugging for short-term camera opportunities."

He hit the nail on the head.

Jackassery is an actual word, meaning foolishness or stupidity. Right on target with these three panderers to the extreme right. They will, of course, get away with it...and encourage others to act likewise, for one simple reason: it plays well to their electoral base, and there are no consequences for such abhorrent, despicable, juvenile, unprofessional and demeaning behavior.

So, the Senate's newly crowned Three Amigos can continue to go merrily forward and bring the institution as the world's greatest deliberative body into disrepute. We can only hope that over time, these three and their willing companions will be relegated to the back bench–much like some members of Congress who, supporting isolationism and railing against all New Deal programs, were forced to silence when World War II broke out and the public mood changed. War and depression will do that.

But it shouldn't take a cataclysmic event to get our highest elected officials to act like adults. Unfortunately, until this happens, we must ask ourselves what kind of example is being set for our children. If this is leadership at the highest level in our country, what does this say about us?

Reminds me of that great line from the Wizard of Oz. You know, the one where Dorothy repeatedly chants "Lions and Tigers and Bears. Oh, my!" Well, we have these three senators:

Cruz, Graham and Hawley. Oh my!

Cruz, Graham and Hawley. Oh my!

TRUMP SUES CLINTON FOR TRYING TO RIG 2016 ELECTION

Here's an interesting story. Former President Trump just filed a multi-million-dollar lawsuit against Hillary Clinton, and others, claiming they conspired to rig the 2016 election by alleging they tried to rig the 2016 US presidential election by tying his campaign to Russia.

If or when Clinton is deposed, she'll undoubtedly rely to some degree on the massive report issued by a Republican-led US Senate committee in August 2020, concluding that Russia used Republican political operative Paul Manafort and the WikiLeaks website to try to help Trump win the 2016 election.

Then there's that Mueller Report that led to Trump's first impeachment.

I wonder what Trump will rely on when he's called to testify under oath. He's been avoiding having to give sworn testimony for years now. But as a plaintiff, it seems he won't be able to avoid that–not that he won't try, of course. The penalty for a plaintiff who refuses to testify is the failure of the case to go forward until he or she does. I have seen cases where a lawsuit is dismissed for repeated failure to testify under this circumstance. And then there's the matter of fees to be paid to the other side.

Perhaps he is just using this to deflect what he anticipates will be coming out of the Congressional investigation into the January 6 attack on the Capitol later this year.

Regardless, I trust his lawyers received a sizeable retainer up front for their representation. Trump isn't exactly known for paying all his legal fees.

This could well be a situation where one must be careful what he wishes for.

"YOU CAN'T MAKE THIS STUFF UP"

Florida's best-selling author and humorist Dave Barry has a famous line he uses to describe something that is virtually impossible to believe. Whenever he discusses something outrageous, outlandish, yet true, he says, "You can't make this stuff up."

This is so apropos to the latest shenanigans that seem to flow from the Republican Party daily. This latest madness can be described as hypocrisy meeting gaslighting joining audacity.

The right-wing senators—most notably Ted Cruz, Lindsey Graham, and Josh Hawley—just completed a circus euphemistically called the Senate confirmation hearing for Federal Appeals Judge Ketanji Brown Jackson. Each senator, along with a few willing cohorts, railed and ranted in their accusations that she was soft on crime. This, from the same senators who somehow still believe that what Donald Trump did on January 6, 2021—another day in American history that will live in infamy—in stoking an attack on the Capitol, leading an insurrection that claimed five lives and injured more than 150 law enforcement officers, was really nothing more than what the Republican National Committee still calls a "legitimate political discourse."

That these senators acted like clowns, feigning moral outrage, gnashing their teeth over a claim that Judge Jackson is soft on crime. Yet, they continue to give a pass to their president and others whose actions took lives, injured dozens, and caused property damage into the millions. This is the height of hypocrisy, and these senators should be ashamed of themselves. But of course, they're not because they don't expect to be held accountable for their actions.

It is also classic gaslighting 101 because they ask you to suspend reality gleaned through your own senses and believe their boldface lies.

For sheer audacity, however, we have news that Supreme Court Justice Clarence Thomas's wife was exchanging email with Trump's Chief of Staff Mark Meadows during the leadup to the January 6 attack. The House committee investigating this insurrection has in its possession those email exchanges in which she repeatedly begs Meadows to overturn the election results. If this doesn't send chills up your spine, nothing will.

You might recall that in January of this year, the Supreme Court upheld a lower court decision that former president Trump could not exert executive privilege to shield records the Select House Committee investigating the attack had been seeking. The vote was 8-1. The dissenting justice was Clarence Thomas!

The logical question that now arises with this latest revelation is what did Justice Thomas know, and when did he know it? Sounds familiar, doesn't it? This was the question asked by Sen. Howard Baker of Richard Nixon during his Watergate scandal almost 50 years ago.

Not to be outdone, it is expected that both Justice Thomas and his wife will deny ever discussing any of this. Those who believe that will believe whatever Cruz, Graham, Hawley, etc., etc., etc., say anyway. But there is that adage that if it looks like a duck, sounds like a duck, and walks like a duck…well, you know the rest. An obvious follow-up question is if Thomas and his wife did discuss this, whether Thomas also apprised other justices of this.

Until this latest shocker, it was generally assumed that those behind the January 6 attack on our Democracy were some in the White House and a few renegade members of Congress. That this scandal might now reach into the sanctum sanctorum of our judiciary, the Supreme Court of the United States, must be a wakeup call for those who cherish Democracy.

Who knows what additional scandalous information will come forth over the next few weeks or months? Soon, however, we will find out just how close we really came to a coup on that fateful day; and we will also learn who the players were and what they did. That pesky truth again that somehow always seems to come out.

Hopefully, we will take what we learn and do whatever is necessary to assure that there can never be a repeat. No more lies. No more hypocrisy. No more denial. No more gaslighting. No more audacity or gall or hubris; no more nonsense. Crime must never pay!

"WORSE THAN WATERGATE"

More than a year ago, Carl Bernstein said the Trump presidency was "worse than Watergate." You will recall that Bernstein is the reporter and author who, with his writing partner Bob Woodward, exposed the Watergate scandal that led to Richard Nixon's resignation almost 50 years ago. Up to that time, Watergate was the worst presidential scandal in American history, and the only one to date that has led to a presidential resignation.

Bernstein was mocked by some on the right for labelling each of Trump's offenses from peccadilloes to the more glaring as the "worst": his ties with Russia, his adoration of despots and dictators, his disdain for our NATO allies, his quid pro quo call to the Ukraine president for dirt on Joe Biden's son, his Big Lie election nonsense, his two impeachments. I could go on and on.

As events continue to unfold, however, it appears more and more likely that Bernstein's pronouncement will be most prophetic.

When he made his statement, Bernstein could not have known that, unlike Watergate, the scope of Trump's scandals would not only affect the executive and legislative branches of our federal government, but would extend its tentacles to the Supreme Court, perhaps even into the Sanctum Santorum itself.

The House Committee on January 6 will no doubt add this latest bit of shock information to its probe, and its members may ask Justice Clarence Thomas's wife, Ginni, to testify about the email exchange with Trump's Chief of Staff Mark Meadows calling for the election of Joe Biden to be overturned. Remember that these are the emails that Meadows voluntarily disclosed to the committee; if these are what he willingly revealed, we can only imagine what additional emails there might be that he hasn't disclosed.

We already have a fairly good idea of those in the executive and legislative branches who aided, abetted, or participated in the both the leadup to January 6, and related events thereafter. Several have refused to testify even when subpoenaed. Steve Bannon and Peter Navarro, who worked for Trump, stonewalled the committee. They aren't alone. In the House, there is House Minority Leader Kevin McCarthy and Jim Jordan who blasted the committee as a partisan hit squad. They are also not alone. That it was McCarthy who tried to block the committee's efforts–and there are still two Republicans on the committee—doesn't seem to matter to him, or the party's rabid base. He has also vowed to shut down the committee when he becomes speaker of the House.

It may well turn out any way that the committee won't need the testimony of the scofflaws who believe they are safe by not testifying. And you can bet the mortgage that when the committee issues its report and names current representatives and senators who were complicit in pressing Trump's Big Lie that led to the insurrection and near coup, each of them will rant and rave about how biased, unfair, etc., etc., etc. the investigation was.

Of course, each will have been given the opportunity to testify and set the record straight. After all, the public is entitled to every man's evidence. The Supreme Court said so. And as Donald Trump famously said about the investigation into Hillary Clinton's misuse of her email account: "If you are not guilty of a crime, what do you need immunity for?" I don't recall him giving this same advice to those who steadfastly refuse to aid a legitimate congressional investigation. Taking Trump's admonition to heart, if these folks have nothing to hide, why do they refuse to testify? Perhaps they should be reminded that executive privilege doesn't apply to criminal activity.

Now there is the matter of the Supreme Court. Thus far, the furor is over Justice Thomas sitting in judgment over cases stemming from the 2020 election. Recall that a judge or justice must avoid even the appearance of impropriety. It's that appearance that compels a judge to recuse himself; however, at the Supreme Court level, recusal is a largely a matter within the discretion of the justice himself.

Under federal law, federal judges, including Supreme Court justices, are supposed to recuse themselves when they previously participated in a case, have a financial interest in it or when a close relative is involved. None of this appears to apply to Justice Thomas, at least so far.

Chief Justice Roberts has recused himself on several occasions because of stock ownership, and former Justice Sandra Day O'Connor also disqualified herself from cases involving telecommunications because she owned stock in AT&T. Other Justices have recused for this reason as well.

Assuming nothing more glaring comes out of this latest revelation, Justice Thomas can, self-servingly so, declare that he can be completely unbiased and not the least bit influenced by his wife's conduct. And if you believe that.....

EQUIVALENCY? WHAT A JOKE!

Whenever a Republican officeholder is caught with his or her hand in the cookie jar, supporters seek out a Democrat equivalency, as if whatever this officeholder did is just as bad as what the Democrat did.

We know that the Republican Party will drop the investigation into the January 6 assault on the Capitol should it gain control of the House. Fortunately, by then we'll have a report that lays out the entire scenario leading up to, and including, that attack. And we know nothing will come of the Ginni and Clarence Thomas situation, either. But they did find their latest version of equivalency: Hunter Biden.

So, let's see. Assuming the worst, is what Biden did equivalent to what happened on January 6, knowing who spearheaded the attack, and who (so far) aided and abetted it? Folks like Reps. Jordan and McCarthy, Sens. Hawley and Cruz, and no doubt many others? And is what Biden did equivalent to what the Thomas couple did? She bought into the Big Lie nonsense, and Justice Thomas has the clear appearance of impropriety. After he was the only justice on the Supreme Court who would have blocked inquiry into Trump's records–raising a clear ethical red flag–will he now recuse himself from cases involving disputes flowing from the 2020 election?

Biden didn't attack the great symbol of our Democracy or undermine the independence or integrity of the judiciary.

Trump, his diehards in Congress and elsewhere, and Justice Thomas and his wife did. This latest effort at deflection is par for the course. It's designed to appeal to the party's base.

Oh, and Biden isn't even an officeholder. The other key players in these two scandals are. Equivalency? What a joke!

THE MYTH THAT A JUDGE'S JOB IS TO CALL BALLS AND STRIKES

Supreme Court Chief Justice John Roberts has repeatedly compared the job of a judge to that of a baseball umpire, saying they don't pitch or bat, they just call balls and strikes.

He relies on this analogy every time the Court is accused of being partisan rather than independent and above the political fray.

I doubt his analogy impresses any senator, for we are now at the point where confirmation depends on which party is in power in the White House and in the Senate. Donald Trump's last two appointees—Justices Kavanaugh and Barrett—were confirmed by a straight party line vote. It appears Joe Biden's appointee—Judge Jackson—will be confirmed in the same manner. Confirmation has gotten away from inquiry into a nominee's qualifications or judicial temperament. Now, it's whether a nominee would "do away with civil rights" on one end, and whether one is "soft on crime" on the other. Whether the hearing process is a circus, or whether the senators engage in rank hypocrisy doesn't matter; it's all about putting on a show to please the diehards.

Senators aren't concerned with balls and strikes; they're concerned about winning the ideological game. To accomplish this, both conservatives and liberals fight tooth and nail to get "their" judges and justices appointed and confirmed.

In baseball, usually one umpire is responsible for each call. The home plate umpire is solely responsible for calling balls and strikes unless in those relatively rare instances when he asks for help. Similarly, each umpire is solely responsible for calls at the bases and in the field, again unless in those rare instances when he asks for help. Then there is instant replay for calls under review. In any event, umpires don't decide the outcome of the game (again except in those rare instances where a call affects the outcome).

In short, when an umpire makes a call, that call stands. He doesn't seek out the opinion of the other umpires on each call. He doesn't confer, caucus, or engage in debate over its propriety.

A Supreme Court justice, however, contributes to the ultimate outcome of every case. The Court is governed by the Rule of Five—the number of justices necessary for a controlling decision. It's about persuasion. Just as lawyers try to persuade the judge by filing legal memos and briefs, Justices also exchange legal memos designed to persuade colleagues to join him or her, all designed to reach that magic number.

Although most cases are decided by a unanimous or clear majority vote, it's the hot-button civil rights or social justice cases that draw the most attention and the closest votes. It's these cases that drive the ideological divide that we see play out more and more during confirmation hearings.

The point here is that each justice is responsible for his or her own disposition of a case. He or she contributes to the outcome by trying to influence colleagues to reach five for a majority opinion.

Judges and justices are deciders; their responsibility is to consider the facts that are supported by the evidence, weigh those facts against the law, and reach a decision based on both.

Without going into the trial and appellate processes, for the most part, judges are called upon to issue a binding decision that must be followed. Only a state Supreme Court can finally and ultimately decide a matter of state constitutional import. Similarly, only the U.S. Supreme Court can finally decide a case on federal constitutional grounds. In fact, that Court is the only federal that can overrule its own precedent and set a new standard or principle that binds all lower federal courts, as well as state courts on issues of federal import.

Can you imagine a baseball umpire with that much authority?

Here is a workable rule of thumb: The Supreme Court's decisions are not final because they're right; they're right because they're final.

WHO REALLY TRIED TO STEAL THE 2020 PRESIDENTIAL ELECTION?

Even before the election results from 2020 were in, Donald Trump, knowing he was behind, began claiming that if he lost, it would be because the election was rigged. Recall that he did this in the leadup to the 2016 election as well. In his mind, this claim shielded him from the risk of being labelled a loser. Donald Trump never loses.

But as revelations continue to mount, it is becoming more and more evident that it wasn't the Democrats that tried to steal the election.

Ask yourself what it would have taken for the Democrats to steal the election. Let's focus on four key states: Arizona, Wisconsin, Georgia, and Pennsylvania. These four had both Democrat and Republican officials presiding over the election in their respective states. These states are separated geographically by thousands of miles. Think of the amount of coordination involved here. Then add in the voting machine company—Dominion—whose machines are in the hands of these diverse officials in states separated by great distances. But we can't stop here. We then must add the judiciary—state and federal judges who would have had to be involved with these state officials and the voting machine company. Think of the enormity of this.

Trump's lawyers filed more than 60 lawsuits contesting the election. Not even one bought into his rigged election claim. Not even one. Aside from bogus evidence and wild conspiracy claims, the lawyers offered nothing of substance to back up their bogus lawsuits.

And don't forget the Supreme Court. Although most of the justices are conservative, all but one (Clarence Thomas, who has his own ethical problems right now–his wife's email exchange with Trump's chief of staff Mark Meadows urging the election be overturned) rejected each of Trump's claims.

To believe Trump's Big Lie, you would have to suspend reality and believe, without a shred of evidence, that a conspiracy unmatched in American history took place before the election to assure that Trump would lose.

One more thing. If this rigging were not planned before the election, try to imagine such a conspiracy being hatched on election day and a few days beyond. Think of how much coordination would be required to even come close to rigging the election.

Yet, even today, there are still those who stubbornly cling to the Big Lie because they believe that Trump is the fount of all truth.

Let's now focus on the election steal from its real source: the right wing of the Republican Party.

Just the other day, we learned from several news sources, including the Washington Post and CBS News, that official White House records show a gap of more than seven hours in the call logs of Donald Trump on January 6, 2021 as violence unfolded on Capitol Hill. (These call logs were part of the records turned over earlier this year by the National Archives to the House select committee investigating the January 6 attack.)

That's a massive gap in communication during a critical time, and now House investigators are looking into whether Trump communicated through other means during those hours – for instance, through burner phones or other people's devices. Trump said he doesn't know what a burner phone is, never heard of it. His former aide John Bolton says otherwise; that Trump used this phrase quite often.

We know that several House and Senate members were in contact with Trump and others in the White House on that fateful day. And we also know these same officials have been steadfast in refusing to testify under oath or provide all relevant documents to the investigating committee. But just from what has been provided to date, we have a fairly good idea of how they were conspiring to keep Trump in power. All that was needed was for then-Vice President Pence to buy into the madness set out in a memo written by John Eastman, a conservative lawyer working with Donald Trump's legal team, in which he outlined a scheme to try to persuade Pence to subvert the Constitution and throw out the 2020 election results on January 6.

As compared to the enormity of a Democratic steal, it would have taken a comparatively few for the Republicans to pull off the steal. Just a VP, a few members of Congress and Republican state legislators just waiting for the word.

Meanwhile, in an interview with JustTheNews, Trump continued a pattern of soliciting foreign help for domestic political affairs when he called on Russian President Vladimir Putin to release any damaging information he has about the Biden family. Recall that Trump repeatedly said he had no help from Russia in 2016. He was impeached for seeking similar help from the Ukraine president.

As the beat goes on, the heat goes up.

TIMIDITY AND NUMBNESS

Two words come to mind that explain where we are politically. One is timidity; the other is numbness.

If there is one word that unites the Democrats and moderate Republicans, it's timidity.

The Democrats are too timid—indeed, almost silent—in the face of revelation after revelation over how close we came to a coup on January 6, 2021.

The rank-and-file mainstream Republicans (however many of them remain) are too timid to call out the off-the-wall craziness of the extreme right wing for fear of angering the party's base and its chief mouthpiece, Donald Trump.

The second word is numbness, and it's what Trump and his acolytes are depending on to get through the mounting multi-layered scandal that broke loose on January 6.

The Democrats are far too timid in their response to what is now a wave of revelations stemming from the assault on the Capitol. They control both the House and Senate, although you would scarcely notice it. House Speaker Nancy Pelosi is rarely seen; Senate Majority Leader Chuck Schumer rarely appears before the media to decry the latest revelation about the extreme right, or even challenge the latest asinine statement from the extremists.

House Minority Leader Kevin McCarthy and Senate Minority Leader Mitch McConnell get so much airtime, you would think they run their respective houses of Congress.

The Democrats' timidity has allowed the Republicans to frame the message, corner the media market, and get away with it by going unchallenged. The Republicans have been so successful at generating fear–framing the Democrats as radical leftists, socialists, and communists—that they are all too willing to allow fascism to enter the home and have a seat at the table. Yet there is silence from the other side.

It seems we are faced daily with another revelation about January 6. We are learning just how extensive the leadup was, and who was involved, in the closest thing to a coup we have ever faced as a nation.

If the shoe were on the other foot and it was the Democrats who launched a coup attempt, the Republicans would have had televised committee hearings stretching into days, weeks, and even months to provide theater and engage and enrage the public. Calls for arrests, charges and trials would have already begun in a cacophony of rants.

Where are those hearings with the Democrats in control of the House investigative committee? They are non-existent.

And where is the nation's attorney general, who is charged with overseeing prosecutions of those who violate the law? I bet a majority of the populace doesn't even know who the attorney general is. It wouldn't surprise me if more people think Bill Barr is still the attorney general. He's been out of office over a year yet gets more media attention than Merrick Garland.

The point here is the Democrats, armed with more scandalous information than Watergate ever revealed, have done just short of nothing to even try to frame a message that is designed to resonate with the public.

Time is not on their side. We are moving into election season, with campaigns, primaries, and the general election just a few months down the road. There will be many competing issues that could easily drown out this most far-reaching and dangerous scandal in American history.

You would think they would learn from the collective yawn that greeted the Mueller Report. Clear evidence of criminal conduct, yet not a single prosecution resulted from what should have been viewed as a blockbuster report.

Not to be outdone, the Republicans have once again set their sights on Hunter Biden, hoping that people will consider the president's son as a perfect foil for their equivalency claims, as if an attempted coup by violence equates to Biden's financial peccadillos, whatever they might be.

The second word is numbness. There is a psychological principle that people initially outraged over aberrant conduct will, despite being bombarded by one shock or indignation after another, become numb. Put another way, people who continue to feel a sense of outrage and anger will, over time, feel so overwhelmed that they become numb to a continued assault, to the point that they will no longer care. In this case, accusations of Trump's many possible crimes and his rants against the Democrats, congressional investigators, and anyone who disagrees with him, already are having a ho-hum effect on the public conscience.

It is time for this congressional investigating committee to use the media to at least try to catch up to the Republicans in messaging the public. No matter how inane some of the comments are from the far right, they get public attention primarily through television but from print media as well. Republicans would rather a message that alarms its supporters and angers its opponents, than no message at all. And the Democrats would appear to prefer no message than a point-by-point attack on ridiculousness.

It's also time for House and Senate majority leaders to use the bully pulpit and their places in their respective chambers to speak to the public. Call out the nonsense. State clearly what the Democrats are for; what the Republicans are trying to accomplish; and how you propose to deal with that.

Timidity is dangerous because, if numbness is allowed to set in and people no longer care about the scandals and possible crimes, it emboldens the scofflaw, and their conduct can be repeated and even become worse.

Moderate Republicans and Democrats must not sit on their hands hoping the public sees the forest through the trees. The public needs to be educated the old-fashioned way; with facts and opinions based on facts, not propaganda, fear-stoking buzzwords, and sinister behavior wrapped in promises of freedom, liberty, justice, law and order.

Don't let January 6 be a dress rehearsal.

PUNISH THEM!

For daring to speak out against the law, Disney faces the wrath of the Florida governor and his compliant legislature. This is straight out of the authoritarian playbook; if you aren't compliant with the demands of the right wing, you are the enemy and must be punished. They have already passed laws to punish those who teach the truth about historical subjects, warts and all; those whose teachings might offend the psychological sensibilities of some folks; they've just about kicked home rule to the curb; relegated academic freedom to the past; made voting like trying to pass a football through a tire at twenty yards; among other draconian laws. All in the name of freedom, liberty, and justice, of course.

Today, it's Disney's turn to face the wrath of the right. Free speech be damned! Besides, that's only for the supporters, the compliant and the silent. For those who speak out about what they believe are bad laws, there is the figurative whipping post.

FREEDOM TO DO WHAT YOU ARE TOLD

Lately, the word "freedom" has been tossed around by conservatives, with the goal of convincing the public that if the Republican Party stands for freedom—and liberty and justice and law and order and whatever soft and fuzzy words they can conjure up—then it must mean the Democrats stand for something else—and that something else must be evil.

But as the accompanying article shows, throughout our history, the two major political parties have used this word with entirely different meanings.

Here is a telling quote from this article:

"Over the past 250 years, the cry for liberty has ...been used by conservatives to defend elite interests. In their view, true freedom is not about collective control over government; it consists in the private enjoyment of one's life and goods. From this perspective, **preserving freedom has little to do with making government accountable to the people.** Democratically elected majorities, conservatives point out, pose just as much, or even more of a threat to personal security and individual right—especially the right to property—as rapacious kings or greedy elites. **This means that freedom can best be preserved by institutions that curb the power of those majorities, or simply by shrinking the sphere of government as much as possible."** (Emphasis added.)

When conservatives talk about freedom, you must ask yourself "freedom for whom" and "freedom to do what?"

To bring this 1984 Orwellian newspeak notion to the present, it's important to consider some vital questions. Such as:

Is a woman free to have an abortion?

Is she free to take contraceptives to avoid having to consider abortion?

Is an academician free to teach about slavery or the Holocaust and engage in a discussion with students that seeks their opinions based on historical facts? This is how students learn to engage in critical thinking, using logic rather than emotion.

Are the teacher and student free to seek out the truth, or must any discussion be outlawed if it makes certain people suffer psychological distress?

Of course, freedom really doesn't mean absolute freedom. You want to drive a car? Better have a license and have passed a test. Want to buy a home? Better read and sign the applicable covenants and bylaws. Want to be a doctor, lawyer, teacher, engineer? Better go to school for a long time and pass lots of tests.

This should prove the obvious: we must all agree to follow certain laws, rules, regulations, standards, etc., that are essential to the existence of an ordered society.

But it is also essential to understand how words are used, for they may have meaning far beyond what you are led to believe.

George Orwell's dystopian novel "1984" serves as the quintessential lesson is how words can be used to mean their opposite. Orwell introduced us to the country of Oceania, and its language, which he called newspeak, an ambiguous language used chiefly in political propaganda where key words have opposite meanings.

Big Brother is the leader; Oceania is governed by four ministries: the Ministry of Truth, which controls news, entertainment, education, and the fine arts; the Ministry of Peace which concerns itself with war; the Ministry of Love, which maintains law and order; and the Ministry of Plenty, which is responsible for economic affairs. These ministries practice doublethink, a process of indoctrination whereby the subject is expected to simultaneously accept two mutually contradictory beliefs as correct, often in opposition to one's own memories or sense of reality.

The so-called Ministry of Truth exemplifies the core message of "1984":

"The name is a misnomer as the Ministry's main purpose is misinformation and falsifying historical events so that they agree with Big Brother. It's the place where lies are manufactured. If Big Brother makes a prediction that turns out to be wrong, the employees of the Ministry correct the record to make it "accurate." The intent is to maintain the illusion that the party is right/absolute. The party cannot ever seem to change its mind or make a mistake as that would imply weakness; so, the Ministry controls the news media by changing history, and changing words in articles about current and past events so that Big Brother and his government are always seen in a good light."

This novel is a classic example of manipulation of the masses via thought control.

Read the last quoted paragraph again and ask yourself this question: does any of this ring a bell?

THE SLAP HEARD 'ROUND THE WORLD

The other night at the Oscars show, actor/comedian Will Smith was enjoying the comedic routine of Chris Rock… until he told a joke that was directed at Jada Smith, Will's wife who is suffering from a condition that causes loss of hair.

Will Smith went up to Rock and slapped him across the face. A few minutes later, Smith won the Oscar for Best Actor.

Since that slap heard 'round the world, Smith has been vilified, the subject of ridicule and scorn. While he subsequently apologized, the Academy is investigating as a prelude to invoking punishment. Some have even suggested that he lose his Oscar or face criminal prosecution.

But what about Chris Rock? At the beginning of his next comedy stint, he was given a hero's welcome.

There is certainly no doubt that there were other and far more effective ways he could have dealt with Rock's using Smith's wife's medical condition as the brunt of a joke. But hindsight is always 20-20. The question is how you would have acted in the moment.

Did Rock do anything wrong? Is he entitled to a hero's welcome, suffering no consequences for his actions while Smith is incurring public wrath?

My father was in show business; he was a comedian during the days of vaudeville. I think I have a pretty good read on humor. There is such a thing as insult humor; Don Rickles made a career out of it. But he knew how far he could go, and he was known throughout the business as a kind, compassionate and giving person. This endeared him to other performers and the public, who knew his shtick was all an act.

Insult humor at the expense of someone's physical or mental condition is quite another matter.

To those who now sit in judgment of Will Smith, ask yourself what you would have done in his situation. Suppose it was your loved one who suffered a significant injury, deformity, or a serious—perhaps even fatal—health condition, and a comedian used her as the brunt of a joke about that condition. How would you react? Put yourself in Smith's shoes: your loved one sitting next to you has just been reduced to a joke in front of a wide audience, and she cringes at the laughter generated at her expense.

It's easy to point fingers when someone else is the subject of abuse. What if it were you, or your loved one?

I'm not going to make any judgment here; that's not my purpose. My purpose is to get those who are in the back seat casting stones to move to the front seat where they're now the target. Then make their judgment.

FEDERAL JUDGE TOSSES FLORIDA'S VOTER RESTRICTION LAW

No doubt DeSantis and his cronies are hoping that the conservative Eleventh Circuit Court of Appeals will reverse. But here's the problem for them. Judge Walker made extensive findings of fact, and appellate courts won't overturn a trial court on findings of fact unless they are clearly erroneous. That is, the Court must find that the trial judge is simply flat-out wrong, despite numerous references to testimony and evidence presented to him. This, as any appellate lawyer will tell you, is an extremely high, virtually insurmountable burden.

Alternatively, assuming the appeals court accepts the facts of the case, the Court would have to rule that the trial judge's legal conclusions are wrong as a matter of law. This is yet another high burden, but perhaps not as high as the first one. Then, there's that presumption of correctness that a trial judge's decision is given on appeal. Taking an appeal is not simply a matter of saying the trial judge is wrong; the appellants must prove that the trial judge committed clear error. But, in this case, even if this decision is upheld, DeSantis and his ilk can always claim they tried to "do the right thing." So, politically, it's a win-win for him and them.

WHEN DID LIBERAL BECOME A DIRTY WORD?

Recently, a few conservative politicians, such as Arizona Governor Doug Ducey, gave a pass to fellow right-wing politicos who attended white nationalist gatherings. According to the Southern Poverty Law Center, these groups espouse white supremacist or white separatist ideologies, often focusing on the alleged inferiority of nonwhites. Groups listed in a variety of other categories—Ku Klux Klan, neo-Confederate, neo-Nazi, racist skinhead—could also be fairly described as white nationalist.

Yet, despite their fellow conservatives' attendance at these gatherings, these politicians said they would rather support their colleagues than any Democrat, because Democrats are far worse. Think of that: elected officials in America saying Democrats are worse than white nationalists!

The questions therefore arise: when did liberal become a dirty word? What makes a liberal (translation: Democrat) worse than a white nationalist? And what would lead elected public officials given the public trust of high office to demean a major political party steeped in our nation's heritage, while supporting, or giving aid and comfort, to these radical groups?

We know what white nationalism is. History is replete with groups that identify themselves as white nationalists. In the recent past, we saw them march in Charlottesville, Virginia, and were involved in the January 6 attack on the Capitol.

But what is it about libcralism that makes it far worse than these groups, at least in the eyes of some Republican officials?

Conservatives typically identify Democrats by their usual array of buzzwords such as radical leftists, socialists, communists, etc.—words that certainly evoke flaming emotions—but as we shall see, whiles these words are full of sound and fury, they signify nothing.

Since these conservative politicians view Democrats as far worse than white nationalist groups, let's look at what liberalism means.

The dictionary defines Liberalism as "a political and moral philosophy based on the rights of the individual, liberty, consent of the governed and equality before the law. Liberals espouse a wide array of views depending on their understanding of these principles, but they generally support individual rights (including civil rights and human rights), liberal democracy, secularism, rule of law, economic and political freedom, freedom of speech, freedom of the press, freedom of religion, private property and a market economy.

Later waves of modern liberal thought and struggle were strongly influenced by the need to expand civil rights. Liberals have advocated gender and racial equality in their drive to promote civil rights and a global civil rights movement in the 20th century achieved several objectives towards both goals. Other goals often accepted by liberals include universal suffrage and universal access to education."

There you have it. This is what liberalism is; this is what it means to be liberal.

From this definition, ask the following:

Is favoring social security worse than white nationalism?

Is favoring Medicare and Medicaid worse than white nationalism?

Is favoring civil rights worse than white nationalism?

Are each of the liberal principles set out in the definition worse than what white nationalism stands for?

These white nationalist groups have been variously described as hate groups. Where is the hate in the definition of liberalism?

Is favoring social security, Medicare, Medicaid, civil rights, voting rights, academic freedom, freedom of speech, freedom of the press, freedom of religion, universal suffrage, universal access to education, and on and on, examples of hate?

Of course not.

What are examples of hate are what we saw in Charlottesville and in Washington, D.C. in the aftermath of the 2020 presidential election.

Words used to demonize unfortunately have that effect, at least in some quarters. What is essential, however, is for the vast majority who know better, to exercise real leadership by calling out the Doug Duceys and stopping them in their tracks. We need real leaders who believe in our Democratic institutions to step up and say loudly and clearly that enough is enough; no more nonsensical vilification, no more spewing hatred and no more lies. It is the informed and educated who must come forth and vigorously refute the dangerous and baseless charges that are 100 percent emotion and zero percent fact, logic, or common sense.

Those public officials who prefer white nationalists over liberals don't deserve to be in public office, stoking fear and advocating hatred over programs designed to help the populace at large. Pandering is not part of their job. Education and real leadership are.

At the end of the day, it's up to the rest of us to help set the record straight, and to elect people of conscience and common sense rather than those who would pander to the worst of us.

TRUMP, DESANTIS…..AND THE CONSTITUTION

Trying to make predictions on politics is a dicey matter, especially with the 2024 presidential election still more than two years away. This year's midterm elections will tell us a lot, but as things stand now, it's safe to predict:

A big re-election for DeSantis as Florida's governor.

A blockbuster congressional committee report that will, among other things, set out Donald Trump's role leading up to January 6 and beyond.

A Republican Party—no, make that a right wing—takeover of both Houses of Congress. And the majority in both houses could be significant.

Once the midterm elections are over, the focus will immediately shift to 2024 and the run for the White House. If Trump completes this year as the perceived leader for his party's nomination, the question then becomes how DeSantis's supporters will deal with the elephant in the room (pun intended).

Trump, who simply cannot lose, might decide to be magnanimous (if that's possible) and withdraw, especially if (1) that congressional committee report is really, really damning and, (2) if the polls show him losing primaries to DeSantis.

A Trump nomination gives the Democrats all the ammunition they believe they need. Four years of gaffes, missteps, embarrassments, impeachments, election lies, and on and on. That won't be enough, but that's for another time.

A DeSantis nomination strips the Democrats of all of Trump's baggage. They will then have to campaign on actual issues, and DeSantis, whatever you might think of him, is an attractive, educated, and articulate person. To Democrats, he's Trumplite; to Republicans, he's a competent spokesman for conservative values, whatever they might be. Besides, the Democrats would be making a big mistake by using this label. DeSantis comes across on TV far better than Trump ever did, and he's not known for making wild gaffes or blatant misstatements.

What about the Democrats? They have Joe Biden, who will be 81 during the next campaign—assuming he runs. And that's a big assumption. If he's facing a Republican Congress hellbent on doing everything that is anti-Democratic Party, his only real power will be the veto pen, and faced with no chance of advancing his Build Back Better program, he might just pull a Lyndon Johnson and announce, sometime in early 2024, that he won't run for re-election.

If Biden chooses this route, timing will be essential. Primaries are taking place earlier and earlier. Therefore, prospective candidates need time to gear up, raise funds, deal with name recognition, and begin to separate themselves from opponents. Timing, therefore, affects Kamala Harris most of all. As the sitting VP, she commands the same seat that George Bush I and Joe Biden had. That's a big push, ordinarily. But how the party faithful view Harris as opposed to other potentials (whoever and wherever they might be), is a matter of some consideration. I'll leave this one to the historians and pundits.

Why is 2024 so important? In addition to setting the policy agenda substantively and through appropriations, a Republican takeover of the executive and legislative branches of the federal government means opportunity to drastically reshape the judiciary. Thus far, it has been the judicial branch that has put the brakes on both executive and legislative excesses. But what if that third branch guardrail were removed?

Constitutional scholars confidently declare that there is only one way to change the Constitution: by amendment; a detailed, convoluted, and lengthy process.

But there is another way that doesn't involve changing a single word: by interpretation.

The United States Supreme Court has reversed its own constitutional precedent over 140 times since our nation's inception, so revision by interpretation is neither novel nor extremely out of the ordinary. Check the history of Plessy v. Ferguson for a graphic example of how this method has been used. Better yet, check the website of the Congressional Research Service for scholarly papers on the Court's overturning its own precedent.

A Republican president will get to nominate all federal judges. With a Republican Senate, those nominees will easily be confirmed (unless they prove to be a colossal embarrassment—as did a few of Trump's nominees). By 2028, Justice Sonja Sotomayor will be 73; Justice Elena Kagan will be 70—certainly not old by judicial standards, but certainly nothing to cavalierly dismiss.

The point here is that not only will a Republican president and Congress make over the trial and appellate judiciary but might well increase conservative control of the Supreme Court.

Which, of course, allows for a much easier path to changing the Constitution by interpretation. Remember the Rule of Five–it only takes five Justices to change the law. Today's civil right might be in the dustbin tomorrow. Think about abortion, gay rights, contraception, and a host of other social and cultural issues that are ripe for target practice.

Some historians have said we are two elections away from a collapse of current institutional guardrails that protect our Democracy—this year's and 2024. Will they be right or wrong? We will find out.

WHAT DO WE KNOW REALLY ABOUT DONALD TRUMP? PLENTY

Until about seven years ago or thereabouts, we knew Donald Trump as a businessman whose success was found on buildings that bore his name, a successful television show, and as an author of a book on making the deal.

Then, he decided to run for the presidency. Although he previously registered as a Democrat, he decided to run as a Republican. Despite never having held public office, he ran against—and beat--many seasoned political figures.

He did this by sounding unlike any major party presidential candidate in at least recent memory. Indeed, I can't think of one who even comes close. He tapped into an underlying but deep-seated resentment of all things that smacked of liberalism. He touched a raw nerve across the nation and ran against the weakest Democratic candidate in recent memory. Many people were tired of Bill and Hillary Clinton and saw Trump as a successful entrepreneur who would bring his acumen and competence into the White House.

Then came his presidency. Although he frequently warred against the press, as well as those who disagreed with him, he was on his way to re-election…until COVID hit. This was his Achilles heel, his weakness, his vulnerability. Each time he appeared at a press conference and commented on this pandemic, he appeared more and more distant and out of touch. Some of his utterances were clearly embarrassing to those closest to him, as well as to some of his more distant supporters.

It wasn't until after he became president that we learned how much he admired authoritarians, dictators, and depots, aligning himself with their strengths; to him, they were strong leaders, the kind hc aspired to be. To accomplish this, he demeaned our nation's allies and railed against Democratic institutions, one after another. The press, the military–nothing and no one was off-limits if they dared to question him.

To him, there was only strong or weak. He was strong; his enemies were weak. Those loyal to him were strong, but only so long as they were loyal to him. Any deviation was a sign of weakness, and in his world, there is no room for the weak.

To him, there are also only winners and losers. He's a winner; his enemies or detractors are losers. In his eyes, he has never lost; in his mind, he's been cheated, lied to, victimized by hoaxes, fake news and other imaginable and unimaginable evils; only he is the vicar of goodness and morality. Remember, his famous words "Only I can fix it."

But now, after all these years, we know a lot about him. He found nothing wrong with his "perfect" phone call asking the Ukraine president for dirt on Joe Biden's son to help him in the 2020 election, in return for releasing congressionally approved funds.

He called his impeachment on this quid pro quo a hit job.

To list his many peccadilloes, gaffes, malaprops, faux pas, outrageous misstatements, and downright lies would take volumes. And this doesn't include possible criminal conduct that we are learning more and more about.

Since his loss in 2020, he tried to overturn the election outcome the extent of which is just now beginning to surface. And so far, what we do know strongly suggests how close we came to Trump engineering a coup. All he needed was for a few more people to shed their decency and moral underpinning in favor of buying into a scenario that never had a scintilla of supporting evidence.

He called his second impeachment another hit job. In his mind, he's the most victimized president in American history. Never mind that he is his own worst enemy.

That so many still support him says a lot about where we are and what must be done to avoid a repetition.

You recall that on January 6, Trump told his crowd of supporters that if they didn't go to the Capitol, they wouldn't have America anymore. What kind of America was he talking about? A pre-Civil War, pre-Depression, pre-World War II, 1950s phony communist witch hunt, anti-civil rights, and anti-voting rights of the 1960s; an America most recently displayed in Charlottesville, Virginia and Washington, D.C. You remember Trump saying there were some "nice" Neo-Nazis after Charlottesville? Freedom of speech and press? Sure, so long as what is said and written is favorable; if not, it's "enemy of the people" time. And just the other day he asked his favorite despot and war criminal, Vladimir Putin, for dirt on Joe Biden's son. This in a nutshell is the kind of America he wants.

Considering what we know about Trump now, it's fair to ask whether the 74 million for voted for him agree with his self-serving rants about the call to Ukraine, the phony "rigged" outcome of the election, the January 6 attack on the capitol, and his pity party victimization railings about hoaxes, hatchet jobs, etc.?

This is important as we move forward because he continues to sound like a candidate in 2024.

We are still learning the extent that he was prepared to go to remain in office. Sell a Big Lie. Instigate a riot. Trample on the Constitution.

Yes, we know a great deal about Donald Trump now. Enough to make final judgments about him. And we will still learn more in the days, weeks, and months ahead–none of which will be positive for him.

The only questions that remain are what are we to make of it all? How many of the 74 million who voted for him in 2020 will simply ignore his behavior and still vote for him in 2024? Will he pick up even more support? And for those who still support him, what plausible rationale do they have for turning a blind eye and deaf ear to Trumpism? With all that we know about Trump, why on earth do they still support him unconditionally?

These are legitimate questions as we go forward, followed by the ultimate question: does he represent what we want America to be?

IS AMERICA THE NEXT EUROPE?

Look at a map of Europe. You will see numerous countries separated not by great land masses or bodies of water, but by a thin line. Each country has its own language; its own politics; its only economic system; its own laws. Geographically, they are neighbors; politically, some are enemies. In present time, we see one invading a next-door neighbor. (Roughly 75% of the Russian population lives in Europe.) Other neighbors are worried, and with good reason. A despot wants more power; he need look only to smaller, weaker neighbors. Once he convinces himself that no one will dare to stop him, well, you know what follows.

Now look at a map of the United States; numerous states also separated by a thin line. The language is for the most part the same, although dialects differ. A New Yorker might have some difficulty conversing with a Mississippian. Each state has its own constitution and laws; its own economy; its own politics. Geographically, the states are neighbors; politically, they've become more like European countries, eyeing one another warily, suspiciously, sometimes angrily.

We recently saw some states actually sue others during the aftermath of the 2020 election.

Based on these similarities alone, it's fair to consider the comparison. But there's more.

One hundred and sixty years ago, we were hardly a united nation. In the Civil War, or War Between the States, neighbor fought against neighbor–in fact, family members fought against each other—over slavery or states' rights, depending on one's point of view. It was not unlike two foreign countries warring against each other over political and social differences.

Therefore, in our own country, we have precedent of neighbor warring against neighbor; much like Europe, where countries historically waged war against neighbors. In fact, it's happening again right now. But there's still more.

When Hitler took over as chancellor of Germany in 1933, his initial plan was to demonize the Jews and inflict economic harm, so he directed a boycott of Jewish businesses. This was followed by increased violence against both Jews and their businesses, leading up to Kristallnacht in 1938. Then came the ultimate in madness, the Holocaust.

Remember this; the first order of authoritarianism is to inflict economic harm on his enemies.

Now, back to our country. Focus on Florida. We have a Republican state government that punishes its opposition through economic harm. School boards and cities that refused to genuflect to the governor's demands faced economic sanctions. Just ask those school superintendents and board members who dared to question the governor's COVID response to vaccines and masks. They were punished for their disobedience. And now, look at the threats being levied against Disney for having the audacity to disagree with the Republicans over "Don't say gay" legislation. The message is, if you disagree and defy authority, you will be punished! You will be made to obey!

This is what's happening in Florida—and will be repeated in other states as well. Florida fancies itself as being a leader among states. Recall the wave that engulfed Republican-led states following 2020 and a defeated president's persistent lies about the results. These red states marched in lockstep to change election laws to make it harder for certain Democratic voters to cast their ballots.

As the examples noted here demonstrate, ratcheting up anger and outrage against the "enemy" works. If one state takes the lead, copycats follow. And Republicans don't want to be followers in the culture war.

An authoritarian knows well that a lie repeated often enough will be the truth to a sizeable number of people. To this day, roughly 20 percent of the voting age population believes Donald Trump ranks as one of our nation's greatest presidents. That should tell you a lot.

According to American essayist and columnist Frank Rich, "History is cyclical, and it would be foolhardy to assume that the culture wars will never return."

It is ironic that, with our nation's history so inextricably tied to Europe and the desire to be independent of that continent, we would be seen today as emulating it in glaring, dangerous ways.

What is the purpose of this brief narrative? It's worth noting that if economic sanctions don't succeed, or aren't as effective in suiting authoritarians, history clearly tells us what follows. More specifically and more recently, European history tells us what follows. We proceed at our peril if we ignore history's harsh lessons.

THE ART OF LYING

Once again, a rabid right-winger has demonstrated that fierce loyalty to the Republican Party's Caesar is more important than the truth. In fact, to far too many, it's all that matters.

The latest example—which will no doubt be quickly supplanted by another lie du jure—is in the form of Michigan Rep. Lisa McClain regaling a crowd of Trump loyalists with the claim that it was her hero that caught Osama Bin Laden.

No. It was Barack Obama. Of course, this won't matter to the crowd seeking greater glory for their leader, and those who want to bask in their leader's aura.

Fortunately, the rest of us know what the current version of the Republican Party stands for.

For the better part of the last six years, we have been bombarded by lies upon lies; so many that they've been categorized, starting with the Big Lie of a rigged presidential election; moving to COVID will be gone in a flash; to a "perfect" call to the president of another country asking for political dirt on his opponent's son; to the January 6 insurrection as "legitimate political discourse." And on and on and on ad infinitum ad nauseam.

They just won't quit.

There is an obvious reason for this. They know the one truth from Vladimir Lenin that "A lie told often enough becomes the truth." A bit later in world history, Nazi propaganda minister Joseph Goebbels reiterated this: "If you repeat a lie often enough it becomes the truth."

For a party that clams the upper hand on freedom, liberty, justice, law and order, yada, yada, its extremists certain keep interesting company with the likes of Lenin and Goebbels providing instruction on lying.

But that doesn't answer the question why the far right insists on revising history through obvious lies. Well, obvious to the rest of us. And here's the answer: They lie because it works! It energizes the party's base that numbers into the millions.

The Republicans have, for the most part, convinced a wide segment of our populace that Democrats are the "them" in their world: they are evil, socialist, communist, radical leftists, and on and on. For the party's base, this is their reality.

Never mind that many of them dutifully receive social security checks, Medicare benefits, perhaps workers' compensation or unemployment compensation. Farmers get financial relief, and don't forget the thousands they received in COVID stimulus payments. Sort of like the bailouts the big corporations received during the last major economic meltdown in 2008.

Each of those benefits listed immediately above is an example of socialist-type programs, many stemming from the New Deal of the 1930s as FDR dealt with the worst economic collapse in our nation's history—so bad historians call it the Great Depression. (We can only wonder what would have been had Hoover beaten FDR in 1932, but that's for the historians.)

Yet, the right wing seems to have no problem accepting benefits from these programs while simultaneously railing against Democrat socialism. Go figure.

As a result of this incessant bombardment of lies, the Republican Party leadership now has tens of millions of loyalists who will believe anything and everything they say. And what they say isn't about carefully and cogently constructed white papers on various policy initiatives, replete with facts and citations to learned references. Oh no. It's about what stokes love and adoration for its leader and dutiful followers. And anger and hatred for the others who represent the "them." This will be the party's campaign theme this year and beyond.

And this will continue until it is stopped. If it's stopped.

WHAT DO WORDS REALLY MEAN?

When conservatives make their pitch, they will invariably claim they are for freedom, leaving the audience to conclude that whoever disagrees with them isn't for freedom…or liberty or justice or whatever other buzzwords they include in the moment.

But what do they really mean by freedom?

According to historian and author Heather Cox Richardson, freedom to them means freedom to pursue "supply side" economics, which puts greater wealth into the hands of the few. Here is a brief quote that reveals the stark reality that when conservatives use this word, it means something far different than it does to liberals and moderates:

"Beginning with the New Deal in the 1930s and reaching into the 1970s, the government regulated business and protected workers and consumers. Those opposed to such a government insisted that such protections hurt their freedom to arrange their businesses as they saw fit. Second to their hatred of regulations was their dislike of the taxes that funded the government bureaucrats who inspected their factories, as well as underpinning social welfare programs."

She further explains that:

Beginning in 1981, the party focused on tax cuts to put more money in the hands of the wealthy, who would, they insisted, use it to expand the economy. Using the government to defend the "demand side," by protecting equality, would destroy the ability of business leaders to arrange the economy in the most productive way possible. It was, Republicans said, "socialism." And so, Republicans focused on cutting regulations and slashing taxes.

Rather than revise their ideology when their "supply side" economics concentrated wealth upward rather than promoting widespread prosperity, the Republicans doubled down on it, promoting deregulation and tax cuts above all else. They have now, in the second generation since Reagan, become convinced that their version of "freedom" is the fundamental principle on which the United States stands and that any challenge to it will destroy the country."

Conservatives are so convinced of the righteousness of their position on freedom that Florida Sen. Rick Scott said in a recent speech:

"Today, we face the greatest danger we have ever faced: The militant left-wing in our country has become the enemy within. The woke Left now controls the Democrat Party. The entire federal government, the news media, academia, big tech, Hollywood, most corporate boardrooms, and now even some of our top military leaders… They want to end the American experiment. They want to replace freedom with control."

These are fiery words, designed to arouse anger and hatred in "them." And it works.

Richardson notes that Scott is wrong historically—not that it matters–but "extremism of the Republican leadership suggests that it is concerned that American voters, including Republican voters, are turning against the ideology of "freedom" that focuses on concentrating wealth on the supply side of the economic equation and would like to see the government try to restore some semblance of equality. This would mean higher taxes on the wealthy."

And conservatives simply can't live with that, as it goes against the very core of their political being.

Sen. Scott, though, says what conservatives believe: if you are against them, you are evil incarnate. Think of their demand on the Pledge of Allegiance. They want everyone to recite it at every opportunity. Why? When they get to the last few words “with liberty and justice for all” what do they really mean?

They’re hoping that when you recite those words, you will internalize them to mean what freedom means to you personally. But judging by their conduct, and Sen. Scott’s “us vs. them” mentality, they mean liberty and justice for all who look, act, sound, think and believe like them. Everyone else is the enemy.

ART IMITATES LIFE

Remember the television show All in the Family? It was a comedy but also a social commentary that ran from 1971 to 1979 and featured four main characters. The lead character, Archie Bunker, was portrayed as a loudmouthed, uneducated bigot who typified every conceivable stereotype. His wife, Edith, was sweet but, well, a few bricks shy of a load. Remember Archie calling her a dingbat?

They and their daughter, Gloria, and her husband, Mike Stivic, all lived in a working-class home. Archie couldn’t avoid the people he disdained. His son-in-law, whom Archie called “Meathead,” was an unemployed student of Polish descent who fit the classic stereotype of a liberal; the Jeffersons next door were black; Edith’s cousin Maude was a feminist (the Jeffersons and Maude had their own spinoff series). Later in the show, Archie’s partners in a local tavern were Jewish.

It was a top-rated show that focused on Archie's rants about all things liberal. The overriding purpose of the show was to see the humor in Archie's rants. (Do you know any Archies?)

Do you remember the opening theme? It went like this:

Boy the way Glen Miller played,
Songs that made the hit parade,
Guys like us we had it made,
Those were the days,
And you know where you were then,
Girls were girls and men were men,
Mister we could use a man like Herbert Hoover again,
Didn't need no welfare states
Everybody pulled his weight,
Gee our old Lasalle ran great,
Those were the days.

The show aired during the latter part of the Vietnam War, after both the civil rights and voting rights acts were passed during President Lyndon Johnson's "Great Society" years. This song was a harkening back to the days of post-World War I to the end of the Roaring 20s.

You recall how the 20s ended: the Great Depression, followed by the greatest wave of social welfare legislation in our nation's history. That wave has never been duplicated because we never faced another economic crisis so deep.

Art does indeed imitate life. Another television example of this is the great Twilight Zone anthologies of the 1960s, written primarily by Rod Serling. who well understood the human condition and human nature. Both All in the Family and the Twilight Zone made us look at ourselves–our anger, our fears, our prejudices.

Today, there are forces that want us to return to the days referenced in the All in the Family theme and demonstrated by the show's main character. These forces champion themselves in the Archie Bunker mode (although they would never admit it) with Mike as the convenient out-of-touch liberal foil.

If history is indeed cyclical and these forces prevail, we can expect a return to those "glory days" of post-World War I to the 20s, and those of the post-World War II era as well.

Remember the House Un American Activities Committee and its efforts to cleanse the federal government, among others, of the Red Menace? This committee wielded its subpoena power as a weapon and called citizens to testify in high-profile hearings. This intimidating atmosphere often produced dramatic but questionable revelations about communists infiltrating American institutions and subversive actions by well-known citizens, particularly in the political, sports and entertainment fields.

HUAC's controversial hearings contributed to the fear, distrust and repression that existed during the anticommunist hysteria of the 1950s. You remember Joseph McCarthy and his communist witch hunt during the infamous Red Scare? How many innocent lives were crushed by the arrogance and shamelessness of one United States senator, with help from HUAC?

Florida has its own sordid history of hysteria during this time. In the 1950s the Florida legislature created an investigation committee named the Johns Committee, after Sen. Charley Johns. This committee was in response to McCarthyism and the Red Scare; its purpose was to root out communists in suspect groups. When this effort fizzled, the committee chose a new target: gay and lesbian teachers and students in Florida's public schools and universities. Over the next four years, nearly 200 Florida teachers' and students' lives were changed forever.

It should be self-evident that neither McCarthyism and HUAC, nor the Johns Committee, were high moments in American history. In fact, they were embarrassing and tragic.

Think these two television shows were all fiction? Think that what is briefly described above following World War II can't happen again? Just the other day, Florida Sen. Rick Scott ranted at the liberal Democrat Party: "Today, we face the greatest danger we have ever faced: The militant left-wing in our country has become the enemy within. The woke Left now controls the Democrat Party. The entire federal government, the news media, academia, big tech, Hollywood, most corporate boardrooms, and now even some of our top military leaders… They want to end the American experiment. They want to replace freedom with control."

Never mind that the Departments of Justice (including the FBI) and Homeland Security have said the greatest domestic threat is posed by radical right-wing extremists. Scott echoes what many in his party truly believe: that he and his cohorts are making America great again and everyone who disagrees with them is the enemy.

Ah yes, a return to the glory days! This is what they want. You can hear their cry: down with the enemy! Let the investigations, witch hunts and character assassinations begin!

TAKE A HIKE

Do you recall Democrat senators walking out of the senate chamber after the votes to confirm Justices Gorsuch, Kavanaugh and Barrett? I don't either. Yet, after the vote to confirm Judge Jackson, all but three Republican senators walked out. These 47 arrogant malcontents showed their disrespect for the process; not that they really care about democratic processes.

One even said Judge Jackson would have defended the Nazis. Of course, several of these juveniles have no difficulty defending, even praising, Putin as he continues his war crimes in Ukraine. But that's ok because these senators are making America great again.

Common courtesy dictates that if you don't agree with applause, you don't applaud. What you don't do is throw a figurative hissy fit and walk out. That's what children do. Well......if the shoe fits!

The sad fact here is that there will be no accountability, no woodshed moment for these supposed adults acting like spoiled brats. They know they have their millions who would blindly follow their every lead and obey any order.

What these senators did was classless and beneath the dignity of public office. But they don't care. Hopefully, the majority who do care will send them a message over time.

Abraham Lincoln spoke of our better angels. I think we'll be ok; sooner or later, those who never really supported our democratic republic will be outed; it happened during the leadup to World War II with the America First crazies; it happened to Joe McCarthy and his mindless minions; it will happen again. The right-wing elements of Republican Party have made no secret of their disdain for our institutional guardrails, and their praise of despots like Putin. Rational people see through the party's bluff and bluster. It will take some stresses, but our nation has been through a lot of trials and tribulations. We'll make it through this one, too.

TIME IS ON WHO'S SIDE?

I think the concern is one of time. We know the House Republicans will dismantle the ongoing congressional investigation, but as President Biden likes to say, here's the deal. The Democrats can read the calendar, too. By the time the Republicans take over Congress (if that indeed actually happens), the committee will have completed its work. The report will have been issued. And the Executive Branch of our federal government will still be in the hands of the Biden Administration for more than two years.

This, of course, includes the Justice Department and, more to the point here, all 93 U.S. attorney offices. They will have more than two years to charge and prosecute lawbreakers. And who knows what the Republicans might do that is self-destructive over this time? Already there are some undercurrents of disagreement. They might just decide to devour one another to save their own skin. Can't say for sure. Meanwhile, the prosecutions will be under way. All in full view of the public. In politics, two years is an eternity. Patience is a virtue.

THE AUTHORITARIAN'S PLAYBOOK—A BRIEF SUMMARY

Historians, journalists, and just about everyone else who offers cogent comments on this subject, generally agree that there are several major points in the authoritarian's playbook.

Editor and reporter Kevin Douglas Grant, who has led reporting projects around the world, generally summarizes these points as follows:

Weaponize Fear–Embrace a language of violence; promote a more punitive culture in an "us vs. them" fashion; leverage sufficient military might. Give opponents reason to believe they'll be harmed—economically at first–if they oppose.

Target Outsiders–Stoke the fires of xenophobia by demonizing immigrants and foreigners—anyone who is different from the "us." Blame domestic problems, including economic woes, on these scapegoats and brand political opponents as supportive or at least sympathetic to these imagined enemies.

Undermine Institutions—Criticize the courts, then take them over by taking over the executive branch of government, whose chief executive will appoint like-minded judges; reduce checks and balances to a concept, not reality; undo established treaties and legislation that limit executive power; weaken protections for free and fair elections.

Rewrite History–Exert control over schools and the media to indoctrinate the public with beliefs that reinforce autocratic power. Rewrite history first by removing references to the nation's warts and failings, including book-banning, and replace it with a sanitized version that includes a heavy dose of nationalism.

Exploit Religion–Appeal to the religious majority while targeting minorities. Conflate national identity with religious identity. Establish that the "us" believes in faith while the "them" are non-believers and therefore bad people.

Divide and Conquer–Use hate speech and encourage violent actors to widen social rifts and manufactured crises to seize more power. Repeatedly remind those who are for "the cause" that violence against "them" is a patriotic act. Repeatedly refer to your efforts as those of righteousness; your opponents are against all that is right and just.

Erode Truth–Attack the press as an "enemy of the people"; dismiss negative reports as "fake news." Counter legitimate information with misinformation, or "alternative facts." Blast the media landscape with endless scandal and contradiction to overwhelm the traditional fail-safe mechanisms. To further erode the truth, add repeated, incessant lying, so that the audience becomes numb to the truth. Remember Nazi chief propagandist Joseph Goebbels' statement: a lie repeated often enough becomes the truth. Use the psychological technique of gaslighting–repeating a false narrative so often that people begin to doubt their own sense of reality or sanity.

Defend Actions in the Name of Freedom—Answer any criticism of these actions as acts of freedom. Include other feel-good buzzwords such as liberty, justice and the promotion of law and order. Attack critics as being against freedom and accompanying feel-goods.

After reading this brief narrative, ask yourself whether any major political party fits any of these points. I think you will.

THE JANUARY 6 PUZZLE IS BECOMING CLEARER

You have been given a puzzle, with pieces scattered hither and yon. Your job is to put those pieces in their proper place, thereby making that puzzle's picture clearer and clearer, until there is no doubt as to what you see.

And so, it is with the congressional committee investigating the January 6 attack on the Capitol as insurrectionists tried to overturn the constitutional process of choosing the president of the United States.

That committee is tasked with gathering evidence—the pieces—and properly fitting them into the puzzle to get a clear, unmistakable picture of what transpired on that fateful day. As with any investigation, the questions that must be answered are the same as those a news reporter asks when gathering a story: who, what, when, where, why and how.

From historian Heather Cox Richardson's column today, we learn that even before the election was called for Biden,

Trump's people knew he would lose. This, from a text message he sent to Trump's Chief of Staff Mark Meadows two days after the election itself.

We know that both Jared Kushner and Ivanka Trump testified before the committee. We also know that critical emails from Trump advisor John Eastman, who laid out a plan that called for Vice President Pence to reject electoral college votes and elect Trump, are with the committee. We also know that a federal judge reviewed these emails and stunningly concluded that it is "more likely than not that President Trump corruptly attempted to obstruct" that January 6 session of Congress. Cox also reports that others have come forth and either have testified or will do so, including members of the Proud Boys and Oath Keepers.

To be sure, there are still pieces to fit. We know that several of Trump's loyal supporters have steadfastly ignored congressional subpoenas and have been joined by others in ranting and raving at a biased, partisan investigation. Many of these same people have shifted their focus on investigating Hunter Biden and Hillary Clinton, whose name seems to appear whenever the January 6 investigation gets too hot.

The **why** is clear: to keep Trump in the White House. Thanks to Donald Trump, Jr., when are getting a firm picture on **when** and **where** the scheme to steal the election was hatched.

Yet to be revealed are **what** exactly took place, the chronology of **how** it unfolded and, most critical of all, **who** was involved. From the latest revelations, what and how appear to be moving toward greater clarity.

Then it will be the who.

It's fair to ask what crimes might be in play.

Sedition is a conspiracy to engage in an unlawful act, such as committing treason or engaging in an insurrection. When at least two people discuss plans to overthrow or take down the government, they are committing sedition.

Obstruction of justice is a crime consisting of obstructing prosecutors, investigators, or other government officials.

A criminal conspiracy exists when "two or more persons conspire either to commit any offense against the United States, or to defraud the United States, or any agency thereof in any manner or for any purpose, and one or more of such persons do any act to effect the object of the conspiracy, each shall be fined under this title or imprisoned not more than five years, or both."

As for the participants, for the time being, ask yourself who have been screaming the loudest in opposition to this investigation. Who have been yelling to investigate Biden and Clinton rather than proceed with the January 6 investigation? Who are most vocal in trying to poison the well by throwing dirt on the investigation and undermining its integrity even before the work is complete?

Then recall this famous quote: "Those who shout the loudest usually have the most to hide."

REPUBLICANS DON'T CARE ABOUT CRITICISM; GET OVER IT! DO SOMETHING ABOUT IT!

Republican senators walked out of the chamber after Judge Ketanji Brown Jackson was confirmed. They simply couldn't tolerate witnessing a round of applause for the first African American female to be confirmed for the Supreme Court.

Republican officials in Florida, not to be outdone, personally attacked Federal District Judge Mark for having the audacity to declare unconstitutional restrictive voting laws designed to make it easier to elect Republicans.

But, as President Biden likes to say, here's the deal. Criticizing Republicans for their boorish, childish actions on display in the Senate, or their efforts to undermine the rule of law by attacking judges, are a waste of time. In fact, criticism of anything and everything they do is a waste of time. They simply don't care. They will either ignore or double down on their aberrant conduct that drew the criticism in the first place.

The fact that adults are supposed to set an example for good behavior doesn't measure with them. As long as they have their base to keep them warm, they simply couldn't give a tinker's dam what their opponents think of their juvenile, tantrum-like actions.

The senators—at least those who weren't at risk of blowing a gasket or bursting a blood vessel during the confirmation hearings—said they voted against her because of her judicial philosophy. You see, she doesn't adopt the originalist method of constitutional interpretation that is the judicial bible for conservative justices. In other words, the senators objected to her because she's not a conservative–as if they fully expected President Biden to give them a seventh seat on the Court after the Justice Breyer retires. They reject the notion generally followed by liberal justices that the Constitution is a living document to be interpreted in keeping with changing attitudes, circumstances, and conditions.

Problem is, there is nothing in the Constitution that explains how it is to be interpreted. Considering the partisanship divide in the Senate, it can be expected that future nominations will be judged not on one's education, experience, American Bar Association recommendation, scholarship, or judicial temperament. Rather, they will be judged solely on whether they are originalists or living constitutionalists.

For those Republican senators who aren't lawyers (and perhaps for a few who are), what this really means is that they will only support a nominee who thinks the Constitution should be interpreted according to the intent of those who wrote it more than 230 years ago.

On the other hand, Democrats will support only a nominee who thinks the Constitution should be interpreted consistent with contemporary times. In short, Democrats won't support a conservative nominee—witness Justices Gorsuch, Kavanaugh and Barrett.

Republicans will nominate and confirm the former, Democrats the latter. If there a party split between the White House and Senate, well, we saw what happened when Barack Obama nominated current Attorney General and former Judge Merrick Garland to the high court, only to have then-Senate Majority Leader Mitch McConnell refuse to even hold a hearing.

This brief narrative should dictate the obvious: criticism of their behavior is like water off a duck's back; it has no effect.

As further proof of this, Florida Gov. Ron DeSantis says there will be a 'COLD WAR' between his state and Georgia if Stacey Abrams wins the gubernatorial election: 'I can't have Castro to my south and Abrams to my north. That'd be a disaster.'

Never mind that Castro no longer runs Cuba, for the Republicans to pass themselves off as the party of compassion and unity, well, again criticism doesn't matter; approval from the base is everything. This from DeSantis is another red meat opportunity for him and them.

Rather than spend useless energy railing at their ill-mannered conduct, Democrats—and the few remaining moderate Republicans who still have a spine—should consider this advice.

The current version of the Republican Party has provided all the ammunition needed to make an informed judgment. And there will be even more shocking revelations forthcoming.

Knowing this, spend your energy focused on getting people registered to vote. Devise a comprehensive plan to assure that they either vote early or make their way to the polls on election day. There should be no excuse for not voting; indeed, there must be none. And in the leadup to election, have a plan in effect that educates the voters on why your plan is better than what the right wing of the Republican Party offers. That should not be a difficult task.

WE HAVE BEEN WARNED

In fact, we have been warned repeatedly over the years. Sinclair Lewis warned us. So did Aldous Huxley, George Orwell, and Ray Bradbury...and others. Rod Serling, too.

The common theme is each of these four authors in their seminal writings is a dystopian society where there is great injustice and pain.

Brave New World by Aldous Huxley, published in 1932, warns against the dangers of technology. His theme is that by using scientific and technological advances to control society, the leaders of totalitarian states will have greater power to change the way human beings think and act.

It Can't Happen Here, by Sinclair Lewis, was published in 1935. It describes the rise of a demagogue who is elected President of the United States after fomenting fear and promising drastic economic and social reforms, while promoting a return to patriotism and "traditional" values. Once elected, he takes complete control of the government via a coup and imposes totalitarian rule with the help of a ruthless paramilitary force, in the manner of European fascists such as Adolf Hitler and Benito Mussolini.

George Orwell's *Animal Farm*, published in 1945, deals with the capacity for ordinary individuals to believe in a revolution even after it has been utterly betrayed. Orwell shows how those in power pervert the democratic promise of the revolution.

Orwell's *1984*, published in 1949, warns of the dangers of totalitarianism, showing the extreme level of control and power possible under a truly totalitarian order. He discusses how such a system would impact the whole of society. One method is the use of words that can have opposite meaning if those in control of government demand it. This language is called Newspeak.

Ray Bradbury's Fahrenheit 451, published in 1953, is about a future American society where books are outlawed, and "firemen" burn any that are found. His overriding theme is the importance of knowledge and identity in a society that can so easily be corrupted by ignorance, censorship, and other devices to distract from the realities of our world.

To these five books, I would add television's Twilight Zone series that ran from 1959 to 1964.

You might have read one of more of these books in high school or college. And you might be familiar with the social commentary of Serling's groundbreaking anthology that presented "ordinary people in extraordinary situations involving futuristic societies, space travel, alien invasions, telepathy, dreams, death and the afterlife, time travel, and cautionary tales of dystopian societies and conformity." You can see re-runs during just about any holiday season, especially around Halloween.

By this time, I hope you see the message of each of these books. They, along with the Twilight Zone series, are considered works of fiction. They could also be considered a warning that what is fiction today can be fact tomorrow. Remember those television shows and movies about travel to the moon and other planets, and space stations orbiting the Earth? They're not the stuff of science fiction anymore.

The themes of each of these books is that of a totalitarian state. They address technology, censorship, book banning and book burning, use of words that have opposite meaning…. you get the message.

There is, however, a deeper, far more profound meaning in these works. Each one is about human nature. The ultimate question they ask is, knowing this, can we rise above it.

But, of course, these books are novels; works of fiction written many, many years ago. They're not relevant today, are they? And besides, as Sinclair Lewis notes, it can't happen here. Right?

We have been warned.

CITIZEN LAWSUITS: THE SLIPPERIEST OF SLOPES

Under Texas law, a private citizen can sue a woman who has an abortion, as well as a provider who performs one. Think about this for a moment. One of the fundamental principles of our system of civil law is that to sue someone, you must prove injury caused by the person being sued, and damages resulting from that injury. That injury is called injury in fact. The question therefore is what injury is a person suffering because of a woman getting an abortion or a doctor performing an abortion? And what damage has been done to that person because of the abortion? The answer is none; but if the courts ultimately allow these private lawsuits, what's to stop a state legislature and governor–in fact, what is to stop Congress and the president–from allowing these private lawsuits for any other situation?

For example, can a state allow for these suits against a teacher or principal for allowing a gay student to participate in school team sports? What about any situation or circumstance that a state legislature deems offensive to religious, moral, or social beliefs, regardless of their merit or sincerity? In short, any hot-button social issue is ripe for this type of lawsuit. Some commentators have called this a form of vigilante justice. It's not hard to imagine the types of lawsuits that can emerge if this form of litigation is validated. Do you think Republicans lawmakers and governors who are behind these bills would be pleased if citizen suits against gun owners and manufacturers were permitted in crimes involving guns?

At a time when we are so divided politically, it seems the last thing we need are laws pitting citizen against citizen. The purpose behind these lawsuits is Machiavellian: by allowing citizen lawsuits instead of the state itself prohibiting abortions (or whatever other conduct might be involved) the belief is that it removes the prospect of the courts declaring these restrictive laws unconstitutional. The notion is that the courts won't invalidate what is purely a private matter, one citizen suing another. Of course, whether our judicial system will tolerate citizen suits on whatever subject can be conjured up by lawmakers and governors remains to be seen. This is among the slipperiest of slopes. The consequences can be drastic and unintended.

ARE SOCIAL SECURITY AND MEDICARE EXAMPLES OF SOCIALIST PROGRAMS?

Whenever the Democrats propose a program that affects the social well-being of millions of Americans, the Republicans predictably rant that it's just another socialist program that is being forced on us. For example, any plan to provide Medicare for All is roundly condemned by the conservatives with the usual pejorative that it's socialism.

When Democrats respond by saying that Social Security and Medicare—as well as other programs run by the federal government–-are forms of socialism, the reaction is they're not because "we pay for them."

Knowing how sensitive this subject is judging by the commentary in the media, let me set try to set the record straight. While it is true that we pay into the funds set aside for Social Security and Medicare, this is beside the point in deciding whether these programs have a socialist underpinning.

Here is a concise description of both major programs:

Social Security is considered a socialist-type program because it is a government-run pension system that cuts out private money managers; that is, the government is involved in the rules, collection, and distribution of funds. The program requires workers and their employers, along with self-employed individuals, to pay into the system throughout their working years. The government controls the money they contribute and decides when and how much they get back after—and if—they reach retirement age

Because the government plays such a dominant role in the Social Security system—deciding how much and when employees and employers pay into the system, how much individuals receive in benefits when they get them, and preventing almost everyone from opting out—it can be said that Social Security is, in effect, a form of democratic socialism. However, it may also be considered a form of social insurance or social safety net.

The bottom line here is that Social Security is, at least, a form of social welfare that ensures that the elderly, disabled workers, and their dependents have some minimum level of income.

Medicare is an insurance program that primarily serves people over 65, whatever their income. It also serves younger disabled people and dialysis patients. Part of costs are paid through deductibles for hospital and other costs.

The government runs Medicare. It sets the prices for use, requires you to pay taxes to fund the program and tracks your earnings and eligibility awhile managing all its revenue. The government runs the official website for Medicare, approves or denies applications, decides which benefits you will receive, and imposes and enforces the program's regulations and restrictions. This is what makes Medicare a socialist-type program.

Neither is a pure socialist program; but to say neither has socialist components because "we pay for them" is simply wrong.

I hope this helps.

WHY IS THE PRESS ROOTING AGAINST BIDEN? I HAVE AN ANSWER

In today's column, historian Heather Cox Richardson asks why is the press rooting against Biden? She lists several the administration's accomplishments that many Americans don't know about. I think I know the answer. Reporting about actual governance is not as tantalizing or jazzy as reporting on scandals, nonsense, and lunacy. Anything that arouses the emotions sells; policies and programs don't. The emotive stuff is on the front page, or at the top of the news; the intricate policy stuff is buried inside the newspaper or much later in the broadcast, if reported at all.

People are not as interested in reading about millions being spent on shoring up our infrastructure or aiding failing businesses; they would rather read about the latest shocking statement from a wacko congressman. The latter reporting keeps names in the news, which is very helpful in an election year. Look, anger sells; I get it. But what about the media's' role in fanning the flames? Should every nonsensical, loony statement be reported just because Congressman Crazy said it? Just sayin'.

POISONING THE WELL

To those who understand logic, you know what this phrase means. Politicians use it frequently. Donald Trump has mastered it. A classic example of poisoning the well is when Trump, well before the 2020 election, said repeatedly that if he lost, it would be because the election was rigged. The well is the election result; the poison is making you believe the election was rigged. The poisoner hopes people will reject the election results for that reason. For poisoning the well, it doesn't matter what the facts are; what matters is having people believe the truth of what is being said.

Poisoning the well occurs when negative irrelevant opinion information is presented ahead of time to discredit an anticipated result or action. It's a technique as old as the hills and is used often for one reason: it works.

All that matters to the poisoner is if enough people accept the poison without question. Today, after more than a year of repeating this Big Lie, and after all that has been disclosed that refutes it, there are still tens of millions who believe Trump. For them, belief is fact, and if enough believe, the lie will be repeated ad nauseum.

Trump used this same technique with the Mueller Report, dissing its findings as a hoax even before it was published. He did it with the COVID vaccine and masks, dissing both as unnecessary and anti-freedom even as they were becoming available to fight the pandemic. To show the strength of belief, even after Trump admitted to taking the vaccine, he was booed by his supporters because their belief was stronger than the scientific facts that led Trump to support the vaccine.

If it were Trump alone, his use of poisoning the well might not have been as successful. Having dutiful cronies buying in to this technique, and using it themselves, no doubt advances the poisoner's cause.

There is also no doubt we see this method used again repeatedly in the leadup to the House committee report on the January 6 attack on the Capitol. In fact, Trump and his supporters have already blasted the committee's work as a partisan hit job. The rhetoric will become more and more inflammatory as we move toward the report's release.

Here are a couple of examples that also make the point:

"My opponent has donated millions to oil companies. He has supported drilling for oil in protected locations. Now, he is going to come and present his energy plan, but let me remind you, he comes as a wolf in sheep's clothing.

At the beginning of a debate, one political candidate says of the other: My opponent has a record of lying and trying to cover her dishonest dealings with a pleasant smile. Don't let her convince you to believe her words."

You see how this works? The well is the opposing candidate; the poison is what is said before that candidate even says one word.

Poisoning the well immediately puts the opponent on the defense, having to prove a negative—that the accusation isn't true or didn't happen. Regarding Trump's Big Lie about the election, his goal was to put those who knew the election was honest on the defensive, forcing them to prove it wasn't rigged.

You see this form of illogic just about every day. "If the Democrats pass this bill, it will bring Socialism to America." "If you elect (candidate), it will put another radical, leftist, socialist, communist, in (Congress or state legislature) who will take away your freedoms."

Whether the issue is Critical Race Theory, indoctrination in schools, etc., all that is necessary is to portray something as evil, and if enough believers buy it, the well has been successfully poisoned. Poisoning the well is akin to a warning: if this happens, this is the reason, and these will be the consequences.

Just the other day, Florida Gov. Ron DeSantis said that if Stacey Abrams wins the Georgia governorship, there will be a "cold war" between the two states. Do you see how this is poisoning the well? The well is a cold war; the poison is if Abrams wins.

DeSantis's comment also says other things, perhaps about gender and race and approach toward governance, but this form of illogic doesn't depend on spelling out the details behind the assertion. The poisoner leaves that for the believers.

All that is necessary for the poisoner to succeed is for enough people to conjure up the evil behind the statement. A rigged election. A mask or vaccine takes away your freedom. A cold war will break out if Abrams wins.

Your task is to recognize when it's being used to influence you, and not be taken in by it. Those who regularly use this technique are hoping that the audience will buy it lock, stock and barrel; that they won't question the falseness of the statement.

It's up to you to prove them wrong.

LETTER TO EDITOR OF FLORIDA BAR NEWS ON JUDICIAL APPEARANCE OF IMPROPRIETY

Dear Editor:

I read with great interest the recent comments in the Bar News by Chief Justice Nathan L. Hecht of the Supreme

Court of Texas, in which he discusses the public's growing lack of confidence in the judiciary.

He cites four reasons for this: politics, the media, foreign misinformation, and the pandemic. The example he uses for politics is the recent confirmation hearings for Justices Kavanaugh and Barrett, and soon-to-be Justice Jackson.

But it's what he fails to mention that drew my attention to the article: conduct of the justices themselves.

First, we have Ginni Thomas, wife of Justice Clarence Thomas, and her efforts to get the 2020 presidential election overturned by unconstitutional means; and Thomas's lone dissent in the Supreme Court's order rejecting Donald Trump's bid to deny the House committee investigating the January 6 assault on the Capitol access to presidential records.

Second, we have Justice Amy Coney Barrett telling an audience: "My goal today is to convince you that this court is not comprised of a bunch of partisan hacks." She said this at an anniversary celebration of the opening of the McConnell Center at the University of Louisville, named after Sen. Mitch McConnell, who sat next to her while she delivered her remarks. We know how influential McConnell has been in getting judges and justices appointed and confirmed.

Typically, whenever criticism is levied, the media are the among the first of the culprits. But the media didn't make more out of these two well-publicized events; they just reported what Ginni Thomas did, and her husband's vote. Equally, the media bear no responsibility for Barrett's comments in that rather interesting setting.

Some pundits say Justice Thomas is not responsible for his wife's actions. That may be true, but it's quite beside the point. Judges are required to avoid even the appearance of impropriety. To believe what these pundits say, you would have to believe that husband and wife never mentioned her efforts, and that they never discussed his vote. To believe there is no relationship between the two is asking a lot from the public. But regardless, it's the appearance of impropriety that Chief Justice Hecht never mentioned.

He was equally silent about Justice Barrett's comments with McConnell sitting next to her. Again, it's about appearance.

It seems to me that if Chief Justice Hecht is going to task himself with offering solutions to the public's diminishing confidence in the judiciary, he should at least consider the actions of some of the members of the nation's highest Court. After all, the justices should be setting the example of judicial independence for the entire judiciary.

THIS IS ON THE DEMOCRATS!

Today, historian Heather Cox Richardson notes two Republican efforts to stonewall and obstruct to back up one Democrat senator's cry that his party must take action. The Republicans have no hidden agenda; their plan is out there for all to see. They are stoking anger because angry people vote. They firmly believe they have the public's support to successfully wage a culture war and roll back individual rights that Democrats fought for since the 1930s.

As Sen. Brian Schatz of Hawaii says: "We have to scream from the rooftops, because this is a battle for the free world now." Right now, the polls show a Republican takeover of both houses of Congress, perhaps with significant majorities. They believe they are in the driver's seat and all they must do is stonewall and obstruct until after the November elections.

It they take over Congress, the Biden Administration will be all but politically dead for the last two years of his term. In the face of the Republicans' seizing the media and the message, the Democrats have yet to offer a concerted counterattack. Time is running short for the Democrats to respond and arouse its base. Policy chatter has thus far been met with a collective yawn. An uninspired electorate is no match for an angry, vengeful one.

Here is one thing the Democrats must do and do now: confirm as many federal judges as there are vacancies. There are 870 federal judgeships that require presidential appointment. Donald Trump appointed 245 federal judges; to date, Joe Biden has appointed 58. There are about 76 vacancies that should be top priority. Sen. Mitch McConnell has already said that he will look at each appointment very carefully if and when he becomes senate majority leader again. Translation: no one gets confirmed unless he is satisfied. Further translation: McConnell will leave courts with vacancies for two years until (he hopes) a Republican is back in the White House and can aid in his efforts to reshape the judiciary into a far-right conservative mold.

As a latest example of Democrat halfhearted efforts to fight fire with fire, the Department of Justice refuses to turn over to the House January 6 investigating committee 15 boxes taken by Trump to Mar-A-Lago when he left office, Th DOJ cites its own investigation, which thus far has produced nothing. Pointedly, the DOJ won't disclose why it can't share information with a congressional committee investigating similar or related conduct. The committee has expressed frustration over the DOJ's intransigence.

The point of Cox's column is the Democrats have yet to find a voice to even begin to counter what is a daily assault on the words we recite by heart at the end of the Pledge of Allegiance: "with liberty and justice for all." The election is just a few months away. Democrats must be loud and passionate in letting all Americans know where we are heading unless the brakes are applied. History tells us. Novels such as "1984," "Brave New World," "Fahrenheit 451," "Animal Farm," and "It Can't Happen Here" also tell us. There is no supposition or guesswork involved here, either by the Republican Party or by the lessons of history, including those set out most graphically in these famous novels. They are works of fiction–right now. They could be words of prophesy tomorrow.

WHY DO DEMOCRATS HAVE PROBLEMS WITH BUSINESS, AND VICE VERSA?

According to recent polls, a majority of the voters believe the country is headed in the wrong direction, and the blame lies with the Biden Administration, and Democrats generally. These polls don't tell us whether the voters prefer the direction we were headed during the previous administration, or when Congress was controlled by the Republican Party.

But with prices rising and frustration growing, it's not a stretch of the imagination for voters to blame the party in power, even if that power is more perception than reality. Recall that even with a majority in both houses of Congress, the Biden Administration's Build Back Better program failed when two Democrat senators decided to buck their party. It is true that employment has taken a hit from the COVID pandemic, with so many changing jobs or simply leaving the work force. This must be factored into the current economic conditions.)

Economists will inform you about the laws of supply and demand, and why prices are rising, and the cost of living is outstripping personal income.

Supply–In laymen's terms, and at the risk of oversimplification, when supply is low and demand is low, prices are low with the hope that a low price will increase demand. When supply is high and demand is low, prices will drop to spur an increase in demand. When supply is low and demand is high, prices will fluctuate as supply tries to meet the demand.

Demand–When demand is great, prices rise. Conversely, when demand is low, prices decline. As demand rises, so do prices. The basic general premise here is that when demand is high, prices will be high.

There is a certain amount of management involved in this economic cycle. Witness the Federal Reserve's setting of interest rates to address inflation. When inflation is too high, the Federal Reserve typically raises interest rates to slow the economy and bring inflation down. When inflation is too low, the Federal Reserve typically lowers interest rates to stimulate the economy and move inflation higher.

It would be a mistake, however, to say that our nation's economy is a purely managed one. We have a mixed economy that works according to an economic system that features characteristics of both capitalism and socialism. A mixed economic system protects some private property and allows a level of economic freedom in the use of capital, but also allows for governments to intervene in economic activities to achieve social aims and for the public good. This is where my question noted above comes into play.

Historically, at least since the 1930s, businesses have not favored the Democrats. Recall that Democrats favor wage-and-hour laws, minimum wage, maximum hours, better working conditions, paid vacation, and retirement benefits, as well as workers' and unemployment compensation, among other worker-oriented benefits.

Businesses are desirous of pleasing shareholders and generating profits. These social programs cut into business income and profits.

Whether it be big corporations or small businesses, the general desire is the same: to enhance the bottom line.

To reach maximum profits, costs must be as low as can be tolerated. This is why there is such a heated debate over proposed minimum wage increase law, and why businesses frown upon any of the other laws listed previously that Democrats favor.

Republicans generally favor a laissez faire system, which is a policy of minimum governmental interference in the economic affairs of individuals and society. They support lower taxes, free market capitalism, deregulation of corporations, and restrictions on labor unions. They frown on social welfare or social services programs, even though about 60 million receive benefits, because they tend to disincentivize individuals without solving their economic problems.

Democrats favor a mixed economy and generally support a progressive tax system, higher minimum wages, Social Security, universal health care, public education, and subsidized housing. They also support infrastructure development and clean energy investments to achieve economic development and job creation.

The economic tension between the two parties drives our politics. Thus, is has always been (at least in our lifetimes) and thus it will always be. Two different world views that give us voters a choice.

HOW DO THE REPUBLICANS CONVINCE VOTERS THAT WE'RE HEADED IN THE WRONG DIRECTION?

Politicians, especially the shrewd ones, know that the public's attention span is very limited, so anything said that arouses emotion is fair game. People hold negative emotions longer than others. Arousing anger, hate, etc., works. The Republicans are far better at this than the Democrats; the latter are more oriented toward policy, which is tedious and boring as compared to the red meat the Republicans toss out just about every day. More people are aroused longer by shouts of "socialism" etc., than infrastructure legislation, for example.

We know that if it hadn't been for Trump's horrible handling of the pandemic, he probably would have been re-elected despite all the other embarrassing things he did over his term. The Republicans no longer must explain why they won't hold hearings for judicial appointments if they gain control of the Senate, for example. We all know why, it just doesn't matter to them anymore, so long as they appeal to their base.

The short of it is when the Republicans are in power, they claim they're preventing Democrats from instituting Socialism, etc. When they're out of power, they blame the Democrats for all ills, including those they created by their intransigence and obstructionism. It's a win-win for them.

WILL THE TRUE CONSERVATIVES PLEASE STAND UP?

This is a fair question, considering that traditional notions of conservativism have taken a back seat to those who call themselves conservative today.

Conservativism is said to have its roots with John Locke, Edmund Burke, and John Adams, with more recent thought exemplified by Barry Goldwater, William F. Buckley, Jr., and Ronald Reagan.

Generally, conservatives believe in personal responsibility, limited government, free markets, individual liberty, the rule of law, traditional American values, and peace through a strong national defense. They believe the government's role should be to provide people the freedom necessary to pursue their own goals. Conservative policies generally emphasize empowerment of the individual to solve problems.

Liberals on the other hand believe in government action to achieve equal opportunity and equality for all. They believe it's the duty of the government to alleviate social ills and to protect civil liberties and individual and human rights. They further believe the role of the government should be to guarantee that no one is in need. Liberal policies generally emphasize the need for the government to solve problems.

Of course, as with the implementation of any general approach to governance, the devil's in the details. This is where the battle lines are drawn between the major political parties.

Goldwater, the Republican Party presidential nominee in 1964, opposed social welfare programs and school integration. He believed that certain issues are best left to the several states. He voted against the Civil Rights Act of 1964; yet despite his conservatism, Goldwater was critical of the religious right, supported gay rights, and defended abortion. He understood that if conservatives are going to support individual liberty and freedom, abortion rights and gay rights had to be included. After retirement from the Senate in 1987, he continued to speak publicly on social issues until his death in 1998.

William F. Buckley, Jr., was an author and social commentator who argued for social values rooted in Christian traditions and against the regulation of business and the economy. He worked to make conservativism more mainstream by, in the words of his son, driving out "the kooks of the movement.

He separated it from the anti-Semites, the isolationists, the John Birchers."

Ronald Reagan made conservativism fashionable and, with charm, charisma, and wit, well, the rest is history.

Considering the sharp divergence between conservatives and liberals in their attitudes toward government and its relationship to the governed, policy differences are considerable. But historically, they have been primarily policy differences.

Then came Newt Gingrich and his Contract for America in the mid-1990s, and the beginning of the rise of what is branded as conservatism today. In the last few years, Donald Trump and Trumpism have taken hold of the Republican Party and emboldened those who began making their way into federal and state governments since the Gingrich revolution.

The question therefore is whether Locke, Burke, Adams. Goldwater, Buckley, and Reagan represent true conservatism, or whether today's version is the true one and properly represented by Trump, as well as current Republican Senators Cruz, Hawley, Paul, Kennedy, Cotton, Graham, etc., and Reps. Jordan, McCarthy, Taylor Greene, Boebert, Gaetz, Cawthorn, Gosar, etc. and Governors Abbott, DeSantis and Ducey, etc.?

Considering what Locke, Burke, Goldwater, Buckley, etc., advocated, as compared with those named immediately above (and others), there is a distinctive clash between traditional conservativism and today's version. This raises several questions. Among them are:

Do conservative principles include approval for an attack on our nation's Capital for the purpose of subverting the Constitution's election process and install an incumbent president upon a lie that the election was rigged?

Why do today's conservatives rail against socialism, yet have no hesitancy accepting social security payments, Medicare benefits, unemployment compensation and workers compensation, farm subsidies, corporate bailouts, COVID stimulus payments, and other forms of socialist-type programs? And why do they have no difficulty supporting authoritarian figures that smack of fascism?

Why do current conservatives who profess hatred for communism and socialism praise and defend Putin?

How does current conservative support for the rule of law square with their efforts to prevent inquiry into the January 6 attack on law enforcement officers and others by right-wing insurrectionists? And why are crimes rates higher in majority conservative states?

Why do so many of these conservatives believe the Democratic Party is worse than white nationalism, whose supporters profess racial, ethnic, and religious hatred?

Why has the Republican Party, which once favored civil and voting rights, now adamantly oppose both?

Why do Republicans routinely accept junk science while rejecting real science?

Do today's conservatives believe in Trump's Big Lie, the "Stop the Steal" movement, Q'Anon conspiracies, and that the January 6 attack is nothing more than, as the Republican National Committee said, "legitimate political discourse?" Why do these conservatives either endorse or remain silent in the face of wild conspiracy theories uttered by their members?

These questions don't reflect policy issues and differences as much as they raise the question of what today's conservatism really is—a radically extreme movement. There are other questions that need to be asked and answered, but let's start with these, and hope we get answers—for the benefit of our country.

Let us hope that true conservatives will stand up and reject the charlatans who appear to have converted it to far-right extremism. Let us hope they will do what Barry Goldwater did by his criticism and support noted above, and what William F. Buckley, Jr., did by ridding the movement of the "kooks."

"HOUSTON, WE HAVE A PROBLEM"

This famous, if a bit altered, quote from Apollo 13 in 1970 could be just as easily applied to our circumstances today, perhaps even more so.

With soaring prices for food, fuel, housing costs, and just about everything else; and with wages not keeping up with high prices, our government is spending its time on non-existent voter fraud, banning abortions, books, and classes, etc., instead of dealing with real problems that affect all of us.

One problem that doesn't even make it in the media these days is something we all experience, and our government leaders don't seem to care about it. It's a nuisance, an annoyance, and for some a serious economic problem.

We live at a time when communications technologies are at their peak and expanding. We can pick up a cell phone (or a landline for the few who still have them) and reach just about anyone anywhere in the world. We can sit at our computer and send an email with attachments with lightning speed around the globe. But our brightest minds can't seem to stem the tide of a daily assault on our senses. I think it's safe to say that you can relate to what I'm about to say.

My wife and I receive half-a-dozen or more phone calls (when we're home; no telling how many we get when we're out and about) and a dozen or more emails oeach day, offering a get-rich-quick scheme, a cure for every real or imagined illness or malady—you get the message. All we must do is call a number or fill out a form that seeks personal financial information and, voila, our problems are solved.

These phone calls come into our landline with a designation such as "unknown," "not provided," "cell phone," or the name of a city we've never visited. Occasionally, there will be a name we don't recognize. We don't answer them. Still, they are an annoyance. Most leave no message; the few messages we get usually begin like this: Halo, Jhorrghe, this is Jhon Smeeth. Congrashulashuns, you are a weener. Please call me as shoon as you can." Well, you get the message here, too. I wonder how many people are fooled by a person named John Smith with an accent from beyond—way beyond—our borders. (The answer: millions.)

I ask this same question when we get emails with reputable logos asking us to call a number for an important voice message—until we check the URL. Thankfully, that's a dead giveaway that it's a scam. But those who are clever—and devious—enough to come up with these schemes will find a way to masquerade these URLs, and then this form of scam will only entrap more innocent people.

It these scams were limited to the Nigerian letter, a scheme in which a sender offers a commission to someone by email to help transfer a large sum of money from some king, prince, potentate, etc., the problem wouldn't be so profound. But they're not.

Scammers are becoming cleverer; their methods more plausible and believable, at least at first glance. They are designed to lure you in, until it's too late to realize you've been had.

These phone calls used to be fair game from 9 to 5. Emails were limited to Monday to Friday. Not anymore. We get calls before 9 and past 7. Emails come in during the weekend now.

Why do these scammers exist? Because they make big bucks. In 2021, scammers bilked Americans to the tune of $5.8 billion—up from $3.4 billion in 2020. You can ask yourself how people can be so gullible as to fall prey to these despicable lowlifes whose job is to fleece; to deprive good folks of their hard-earned savings.

It's the classic, toxic combination of greed and gullibility. Recall American showman P.T. Barnum's famous statement that there's a sucker born every minute. Recall the days of the carnival hucksters: the degree of sophistication is all that's changed. It's still all about the two big G's. All that is necessary for scammers to succeed is to add gullibility with the desire to get rich quick. Then mix that combo with greed, the desire to accumulate more at the expense of others, regardless of the chosen means.

It's good for folks to recall the admonition that if it sounds too good to be true it probably is. But that get-rich-quick lure kicks in, and the gullible convince themselves they're smart enough to know a fraud from the real deal. And the greedy play them like a violin.

Considering its growth, the seriousness of this problem can't be overestimated. Americans are losing billions each year.

Meanwhile, our government is too busy waging a culture war to be bothered by this and other real problems that beset us.

"WHAT ARE YOU GOING TO DO ABOUT IT?"

With all the criticism directed at the Republican Party; with all the vitriol and anger against their unconstitutional un-Democratic actions, the former GOP has one very important factor on its side: a firm belief that there isn't thing their critics can do about it.

Accuse the Republicans of right-wing extremism? So what? The party leaders have their base that believes they are the victims of a slide toward socialism and communism. Red meat works. Anger works. And if enough voters are riled up and ready to vote against anything that smacks of Democrats, they're ready, willing, and able to heed the call.

"Republicans are trampling on the Constitution." Ok, so what? Going to take them to court? Have you noticed a shift in the judiciary over the past few years? Sure, there are still plenty of Democrat appointees at the trial level; but look at the appellate courts, federal and state. That's where the rubber meets the road. Look at Florida Gov. Ron DeSantis's efforts to change voting laws, classroom instruction, academic freedom, abortion rights, etc. He knows he's going to lose in federal district court, and perhaps in state appellate court, but the Eleventh Circuit Court of Appeals, and the state and federal Supreme Courts are loaded with Republican appointees. Think he and his fellow governors are worried about the threat of going to court? Nada!

"We'll vote them out." Ok, great idea. All you must do is mobilize your voters to take all necessary steps to overcome the difficulties imposed by all the new voter registration and polling laws designed specifically to elect Republicans. They are well aware of historic voting patterns. Their legislation—passed under the nonexistent notion of eliminating voter fraud–-is targeted to those voting patterns. And enforcement of these restrictive laws is squarely in the hands of their election police squads. Good luck at the polls.

"We'll protest peacefully." Ok, that's good. Only if some police officer thinks you're a bit too vocal, you'll be arrested under those new laws that are designed to restrict protests. What is one person's peaceful protest is another's violent protest. Kind of like eye of the beholder stuff, you know. And if arrested, you'll go before a judge who may or may not be sympathetic. And if you get a bad ruling, well, there's always the appellate courts, right? See third paragraph above.

The Republicans have been itching for this power scenario for years. Their view of the Constitution and its promise of equality and liberty are quite different from that of the Democrats. While both parties claim to stand for the same principles of liberty, freedom, and justices, they differ markedly in how they are exemplified. The inter-party battle we are witnessing today is not new, provided you understand history.

Right now, Democracy is taking a back seat to authoritarianism. Authoritarians believe that people are not fully capable of governing themselves; they need a strong, assertive leader to guide them. The notion is that guidance is needed so the people can be free to provide for themselves. Again, the devil's in the details, and we know from the days of an unregulated America who gets the cake and who gets the crumbs.

The only way to change is to vote 'em out. Yes, it will be difficult because voting has been made more difficult. But this is important: the right wing is a minority; most people favor Democracy. If all necessary efforts are made to select candidates who believe in those principles that undergird our country, campaign vigorously for them, and then vote for them either via early voting, by mail (where allowed) and at the polls on election day, the right wing can be silenced as they were before.

Understand, however, that the right wing has been both in the forefront of American policy as well as silenced; just look to the period leading up to World War II. Recall the America First Committee that favored isolation and negotiations with Hitler, until Japan attacked Pearl Harbor. While the committee went silent, its extreme conservative belief system has always been here. Its progeny is what we're dealing with today.

Recall Ben Franklin's comment at the conclusion of the Constitutional Convention in 1787. Legend has it a woman asked him a question as he left Independence Hall: "Doctor, what have we got? A republic or a monarchy?" Franklin supposedly replied, "A republic, if you can keep it." He also said: "Our new Constitution is now established, everything seems to promise it will be durable; but, in this world, nothing is certain except death and taxes."

We are the current standard-bearers of its durability. We are the ones who are called upon to answer the challenge of whether we can keep our republic.

To be sure, many heretofore nonexistent obstacles have been tossed in our path. Our job is to step over them, around them and by them, and always remain vigilant to avoid them in the future.

AUTHORITARIANISM WORKS FOR MANY, BUT THERE IS A HEAVY PRICE TO PAY

It seems that for many, an authoritarian form of government—a dictatorship—is preferred to a democracy. A "one-man rule" form of government, however, comes with a heavy price. Those of us who understand history know what that price is. The question is whether those who still strongly support Trump or any of his authoritarian-supporting acolytes like Ron DeSantis know what that price is.

Briefly, authoritarianism is characterized by highly concentrated and centralized government power maintained by political repression and the exclusion of potential challengers. It uses political parties and mass organizations to mobilize people around the goals of the regime.

Does this definition strike a chord with you? Do you see anything here that seems familiar? You had better.

You see, an authoritarian, regardless of type (socialist, fascist, Nazi, communist, etc.), must be supreme, which means no one can doubt him. He must be considered infallible. The dictator must never be seen as weak; he is never at fault. A dictator can't be supreme, his every word law, if he's considered weak or fallible. He never makes mistakes. For a dictator, arrogance is a way of life.

For a dictator to succeed, however, he must have a willing group of obedient followers or sycophants doing his every bidding without question. He must also have a "them"—a clearly identified "enemy" he can blame for all the nation's troubles. So long as Mr. Dictator has his lemmings and an identifiable enemy, he's got it made.... provided his followers (meaning the citizenry) stay in line. Dissent or disagreement in any form or manner is not—and will not be—tolerated.

To enjoy a dictator form of government, you must agree with everything—EVERYTHING—the dictator says and does. Read that line again.

If anyone dares to doubt, question, or criticize Mr. Dictator, that person becomes part of the "them"—the enemy he must have to assure absolute control. With that clearly defined enemy, Mr. Dictator can arouse his blind supporters into venting their wrath at "them," the true enemy of the people....as defined by him.

The "enemy" takes many forms (the media, the liberals, anyone who disagrees with the supreme authority), and we hear a daily cacophony of emotive labels coming forth from the extreme right defining the enemy of the day. This is designed to keep the True Believers angry at the "them" so that whatever the dictator wants to do, he can do so without question.

We don't need to look very far to see how a dictator treats former friends and supporters who dare to question or doubt him. Look how many of Trump's early supporters have joined the enemies list for having the audacity to question him? Nobody dares to question Big Brother; to do so means punishment.

And for evidence of this, look no further than Florida Gov. Rick DeSantis and his legislative lemmings. For daring to question him, DeSantis pushed through legislation punishing Disneyworld. Those punished, however, will be homeowners who will see their property taxes skyrocket, and workers who will lose jobs and leave the area, which will no doubt depress the local economy. Those consequences, however, are not nearly as important as sending the message that disagreement will lead to punishment. In this case, DeSantis has delivered his message that the tourism industry is not above being taken to task for disagreeing with Big

Ron.

The thing of it is this kind of demagogic behavior can't be chalked up to stupidity or ignorance. While Trump repeatedly demonstrated a lack of intelligence, believing in his gut rather than his brains, others of a similar ilk can't be so easily dismissed.

Sen. Ted Cruz is a well-educated man, although he has flashes of stupidity. DeSantis is similarly a well-educated man. Unlike Trump, they are also True Believers who believe that our democracy has given way toward socialism and that to take our nation back to the "good old days," we need an authoritarian in charge to assure our freedom, liberty, and rule of law.

History shows, however, that they mean freedom, liberty, and rule of law as defined by the dictator and enforced by him and his lemmings. The phrase "You are free to do as we tell you" is a most appropriate in how a dictator uses calming, reassuring words to mask their true meaning.

Tragically, history shows that by the time the masses woke up and realized they've been had, it was too late…too much damage, hurt and pain had been caused. Look back no further than World War II.

Just look at Hitler's Germany, Italy's Mussolini, and the general history of dictators and despots. All the evidence is right there in the books. All that is necessary is to read and compare to today's conditions in our country.

History does repeat itself. We know that. The real question is what we are to do about it before events control us and we reach a point of no return.

THE MARK OF THE TYRANT

History is replete with tyrants, despots, and murderers. From Genghis Khan, Attila the Hun, Bloody Mary, etc., to Lenin, Mao, Hitler, Stalin, Pol Pot, Kim II Sung, Idi Amin, Milosevic, etc., all had one thing in common: they evoked fear in their citizenry.

They believed in their divine right to govern as they saw fit.

They believed in their self-righteousness and tolerated no dissent.

They demonized their opposition as enemies of the people.

They had sycophants who blindly and willingly bent to their will.

And they punished those who didn't agree with them.

Any of this ring a bell?

KANYE WEST HAS WON 22 GRAMMYS. HOW RELEVANT IS THE GRAMMY?

Music is all about personal taste. Since the Grammys were first awarded in 1959, Elvis Presley has won 3; Elton John 6; Celine Dion 5 and Madonna 7.

The Beatles won 4 Grammys while together; the Rolling Stones 3.

Those who never won a Grammy include Diana Ross, the Beach Boys, Sammy Davis, Jr., and Dean Martin.

This, to me, demonstrates that winning Grammys is not about musical greatness. Not even close. The names of Presley, John, Madonna–and others–will be remembered as long as there is music. Kanye West?

A BADGE OF HONOR, A BADGE OF DISGRACE

Right wing advocates are called nuts, kooks, crazy, lunatics, and on and on. Epithets like these mean nothing to them; they think the same about Democrats. To the right-wing extremists, these descriptions are worn like a badge of honor. Incredibly, although the word "woke" means aware or cognizant, they have perverted this word and proudly consider themselves "anti-woke," or proudly ignorant or indifferent.

Judging from recent social media posts, there are still millions who, despite what we've learned over the past 18 months—and what we will learn going forward--believe the presidential election was rigged; that Trump and his ilk are misunderstood victims of the liberal media and pundits. They also believe those who attacked the Capital on January 6, 2021, were radical left-wingers dressed up to look like Trump supporters. This, despite testimony from those who are now convicted felons who testified that they were doing what Trump told them to do. For the right-wing fanatics, however, truth takes a back seat to belief.

In short, there are people out there who will believe anything. To them, Trump and his acolytes can do no wrong; the problems are those evil Democrat liberal left-wing socialists/communists who want to tear down our country. Never mind that the authoritarianism they seek will tear down our country.

Hannah Arendt, in “The Origins of Totalitarianism,” explains how a strategy of falsehoods and conspiracy aids autocratic movements:

“The totalitarian (or authoritarian) ….. leader bases (his) propaganda on the correct psychological assumption that under such conditions, one could make people believe the most fantastic statements one day, and trust that if the next day they were given irrefutably proof of their falsehood, they would take refuge in cynicism; instead of deserting the leaders who had lied to them, they would protest that they had known all along that the statement was a lie and would admire the leaders for their superior tactical cleverness.”

Oliver Hahl, Minjae Kim, Ezra W. Zuckerman Sivan, in “The Authentic Appeal of the Lying Demagogue: Proclaiming the Deeper Truth about Political Illegitimacy,” support this view of the totalitarian, or authoritarian, pointing out that those who want to destroy what they think of as the “political establishment” willingly embrace lies. In a Putin-style regime, state-controlled media normalizes the leader’s constantly changing stories, which further obliterate any notion of a shared truth. Without a shared truth, or factuality, the rule of law and eventually democracy itself become impossible.

Authoritarianism, regardless of type, nevertheless is perfectly fine for the extreme right because they’re fighting against left-wing extremism; the end justifies the means. They don’t care that history shows this “left-wing extremism" in the form of the New Deal helped us move on from the Great Depression, caused in part by a laissez faire governmental attitude toward business. Remember Calvin Coolidge's "the chief business of the America people is business" pledge? Nothing here about wages and hours, working conditions, etc. For the laissez faire group, it was—and remains—all about business. This means Big Business—and the oligarchs who must maintain and even expand their wealth through a system rigged in their favor. It's called corporate welfare.

The conservatives are in the process of dismantling the social network that has sustained our nation for almost 100 years. History tells us what will happen if they are successful; but again, history doesn't matter to them. In fact, they're too busy re-writing it.

The right wing has become so brazen, they have thumbed their noses at any pretense of accountability. Donald Trump, their supreme ringleader, thumbs his nose at a judge who cites him for contempt for thumbing his nose at a subpoena.

Others have thumbed their noses at congressional and court-issued subpoenas. Yet, despite this, it is clear that Trump, former Trump Chief of Staff Mark Meadows, and several current members of Congress, are implicated in the January 6 assault on the nation's Capital, yet they continue to stonewall and cast blame everywhere but upon themselves.

Richard Nixon got caught in a lie. Donald Trump got caught in many lies. Kevin McCarthy is just the latest to get caught–-he denied that he was prepared to tell Trump to resign during the January 6 attack and predictably blamed the media—until a tape recording showed him to be a liar. He then begged forgiveness from Trump, and the latter's blessing. So much for showing some spine. The simple fact is, however, that liars do get caught.

The congressional committee investigating that assault is making it plainly clear to those who care that more than just a handful of renegades were involved in an assault on democracy. We continue to learn how precariously close we came to a coup.

These lawbreakers must be called out for what they really are. They are not supporters of law and order; unless it's their version of law and order. They are not for liberty or freedom unless they have control over how liberty and freedom are to be defined and implemented.

They rant about socialism but have no trouble advocating authoritarianism in the form of fascism. They avoid the historical fact that our nation has a form of socialist-type programs and has had it since the 1930s. They also avoid mentioning the fact that many who rail against socialism take advantage of its benefits, such as social security, Medicare, and corporate welfare in the form of tax benefits. America's oligarchy simply wants to keep it that way for themselves and toss a bone or two to the rest.

Notice how some on the far right who rail against socialism and communism nevertheless give their support to Putin. Their support for democracy by wrapping themselves in the American Flag would be laughable if the consequences weren't so dire.

How are these scofflaws to be called out? By indictment, prosecution, conviction, and imprisonment. This is how we have consistently dealt with lawbreakers.

If we are to continue to be a nation of laws, then those responsible for January 6—and we know who they are—must be held accountable.

Until that happens, they will continue to thumb their noses at lawful authority, trample on the Constitution while claiming to defend it, and wear all the epithets levelled against them as a badge of honor.

It is up to the rest of us to make certain that this badge becomes a badge of disgrace.

DON'T THINK, JUST REACT

The classic Republican Party line goes something like this: The Democrat Party has been taken over by radical left-wing extremists. If these liberals have their way, they will bring socialism to our country and take away all our freedoms.

The hoped-for (and far too typical) reaction from the party faithful is one of anger, resentment, and hatred. The right-wing loyalists are asked—begged—not to think, just react viscerally against all things liberal.

Unspoken, but just as relevant is the party's corollary statement that goes something like this: To prevent a socialist takeover, our nation needs a strong leader (translation: fascist-type authoritarian), a supportive legislature (translation: rubber-stamping sycophants) and a judiciary that understands that the law is to be interpreted as written (translation: a compliant judiciary that backs the boss).

Again, thinking, and rational judgment are not required. In fact, they work against efforts at demonizing opposition and acceptance of an authoritarian, genuflective legislature and judiciary as the only feasible alternative to socialism.

It is not difficult to conjure up all possible evils when hearing the word "socialism," but what exactly is it? A short definition will suffice: A common definition is that socialism is "an economic and social policy in which the public owns industry and products, rather than private individuals or corporations. Under socialism, the government controls most means of production and natural resources, among other industries, and everyone in the country is entitled to an equitable share according to their contribution to society. Individual private ownership is encouraged.

Politically, socialist countries tend to be multi-party with democratic elections. Currently no country operates under a

100% socialist policy. Denmark, Iceland, Finland, Norway, and Sweden, while heavily socialist, all combine socialism with capitalism."

Read that line again: Not a single country in the world operates as a complete socialist government.

As Jack Schwartz, the late Newsday book editor and author explained, the Socialist Party platform of 1912 contained many policies Americans now wouldn't think of as "socialist," including: "An eight-hour workday at a decent wage, a public-works program for the jobless (realized later in the New Deal's Works Progress Administration), safety regulations for workers in the mines and factories, a child-labor law, an old-age pension, unemployment and accident insurance, a graduated income tax, an inheritance tax, suffrage for women, a direct vote in national elections doing away with the electoral college, the creation of separate departments of health, education and labor, and a convention to revise the Constitution. The first of their political demands was absolute freedom of the press, speech, and assembly."

Again, the Republican Party doesn't expect you to think through its socialism statement; only anger, resentment, and hatred will do. Once people buy the myth that America is headed toward socialism, the shift to fascism as the alternative isn't that far-fetched.

As for giving up all those freedoms, the fact is we live in a well-regulated society. Try driving a car without insurance or refusing to pay property taxes that help fund public schools because you don't have a child in those schools. I could recite example after example, but the message is clear…or certainly should be once thought is given to such things. Just think for a moment about what you do each day that doesn't involve some form of government regulation. Oh, there's that word again, that pesky "think." The Republicans don't want you to do that.

They also don't want you to think about what our nation would be like under an authoritarian, fascist-type ruler. A one-man rule with a compliant legislature and judiciary doesn't work unless most if not all vestiges of freedom are sacrificed. The authoritarian requires complete control without question. He may promise much, but once in power, freedom is what the ruler says it is. Just think about dictators of relatively recent vintage: Adolf Hitler, Benito Mussolini, Idi Amin, Pol Pot, Josef Stalin, etc. History tells us what they promised their citizens, and what they really received.

But, yet again, thinking about these things is contrary to the Republican Party's playbook.

Thinking, however, separates us from lower forms of mammals. It allows us to separate fact from fiction, reality from BS. If people give in to blind reaction and forgo thinking—critical analysis, rational judgment, etc., –what does that say about them? And what does it say about those elected and appointed officials who stoke anger, resentment, and hatred and don't want you to think?

THE DEMOCRATS ARE NOT GETTING THE MESSAGE

Leave it to the Democrats to snatch defeat out of the jaws of victory. The Republicans are far better at knowing what sells: fear, anger, resentment, etc. When folks say they're worried about crime, the Republicans talk about more guns and "constitutional carry;" the Democrats talk about taking guns away from law-abiding people. Which sells better? Since far too many don't learn from history, why should we expect a November thrashing to make any difference to the Democrats? Sure, there's a lot of craziness from the Republicans, and they've certainly skewed election laws and legislative and congressional seats in their favor, but they're in the media every day and, in politics, publicity counts.

When folks like McConnell, McCarthy, etc., get more press play than Pelosi, Schumer, who are the leaders of both houses, what does that say about the Democrats? I get solicitations every day from James Carville, among others, asking for money, as if that will cure all the party's ills. The party needs a top-to-bottom overhaul that eliminates groupthink and focuses on the concerns, fears, needs, etc. of real people who go to work, pay their bills, etc. Of course, there is a real fear of what a Republican takeover will mean, especially for 2024 and beyond. But people have short memory spans, and 2024 is not on the public's radar right now. The Democrats had better wake up, and time isn't on their side.

YOU WILL BE PUNISHED!!!

Disney learned its lesson the hard way: for authoritarian dictator wannabees like Donald Trump and Ron DeSantis, loyalty is a one-way street. So long as you support everything they say and do, or remain silent, you're on their good side. But should you question or disagree, you become the enemy and, to set an example for others, you must be punished.

For business owners (and others) out there, remember this harsh lesson Disney has now learned: if you donate and later disagree with the leader, you will be punished for having the audacity to challenge he who must be obeyed.

But of course, since we don't seem to learn important lessons from history, there will be those who believe that seeking favor by donating to one's campaign will forever endear them to their leader once elected. That works—providing they can accurately predict the future, and that they can, without reservation, commit that they will never change their views no matter what the leader says or does.

Predicting the future, however, is risky crapshoot. Disney donated to DeSantis for the same reasons people donate to candidates generally: donors support the candidate's stand on the issues and want the leader to look with favor on whatever the donor might want from government. The latter is the more plausible reason. You think people donate hundreds of thousands of dollars solely for "good government?"

But then DeSantis took a stand on "Don't Say Gay." Disney disagreed with DeSantis and then committed the unforgivable crime of taking that disagreement public. Big mistake. The authoritarian's cardinal rule is he must never be challenged or made to appear fallible or weak. Criticism does precisely that. The result of such horrendous behavior requires severe punishment.

Perhaps Disney believes it was perfectly ok to disagree because, well, there's that First Amendment which prohibits government from making a law prohibiting free speech. Well, that's the law now; who knows what "the law" will be once the conservative-dominated Supreme Court decides to take up this case, or one like it. Remember, it only takes five justices to say what the Constitution means.

There is a different, but related, issue at play here; one that doesn't require a leap in logic to understand. With accusations of socialist, communist, fascist, Nazi, etc., being bandied around freely, for the purpose of understanding right wing authoritarianism, it's important to discern the distinction between fascism and Nazism. Both are based on the concept of one-man rule; however, Nazism is premised on a belief in the superiority of the Aryan race. Nazis embrace such concepts as eugenics (which discouraged, for example, "reproduction by persons having genetic defects or presumed to have inheritable undesirable traits") and scientific racism to further their views. Nazism views the state as the means to perpetuate these racist views.

It has been reported that Russian Foreign Minister Sergei Lavrov claimed that Hitler was part-Jewish. Pointedly, he offered no facts to support this, and admitted he could be wrong. But that doesn't matter; such a ludicrous notion that a Jew is responsible for killing six million Jews is out there for those who buy crazy conspiracy theories and will therefore believe just about anything regardless of its extremity. This statement was not made in isolation; he would not have said without Vladimir Putin's stamp of approval.

This is an unmistakable effort on Russia's part to somehow excuse or delegitimize the Holocaust.

Here is why this matters. According to the playbook, the authoritarian convinces his audience that "the enemy" is responsible for all evils and pain. He then promises to restore love, peace, liberty, freedom, justice, etc. if he becomes the chosen one. But once chosen and in power, he must remain in power. He does this in part by a careful, cultivated demonization of "the enemy."

It is not a stretch for an authoritarian to set his sights on history's convenient scapegoat. Recall a recent president who said there were some nice Neo-Nazis who took part in the Charlottesville, Virginia, "Unite the Right" demonstration in 2017. Presumably, there are others like him who agree that there are some nice Neo-Nazis.

We know that some extreme right-wing Republicans support Putin, whose stated purpose in attacking Ukraine is to de-Nazify that country, even though its president is Jewish. Sadly, this kind of topsy turvy Newspeak appeals to the gullible.

The question becomes how do we stop the slide toward authoritarianism before it descends into the type of madness and darkness that was Europe during World War II? The potential inevitability of this slide is there for all to see. It's in our history books. All we must do is pay heed to it. And act to prevent it.

JANUARY 20, 2025. THE PRESIDENT'S INAUGURAL ADDRESS

My fellow Americans, today is a new day for our great country. Today, we show the world what a united America looks like. We are united in purpose and spirit. We speak with one voice; we hold one set of values and ideas.

We are the beacon of freedom, liberty, and justice, the only true light in an otherwise dark and dangerous world. God has ordained us to be this true beacon of light and right, and we must not waver or fail in our mission to show the world what it means to be an American.

America can be great only if all who call themselves true American patriots unite behind our government.

Two years ago, you spoke in an unmistakable manner when you by your overwhelming vote chose strong Republican leadership to take charge of Congress. You reiterated that great support by your vote this past November.

By your vote in 2024, we the party faithful are now on the precipice of true American greatness.

The sacred words "with liberty and justice for all" means just that—for all true, loyal Americans who fervently believe in our nation's greatness.

But over the past several decades, we have seen the foundation of our great nation undermined by actions that smack of a different and evil type of government–socialism. We have seen our precious freedoms perverted by giveaway programs that erode the strength of the individual. Slowly but surely, your freedoms have been taken from you.

Today, we begin to take them back.

Today, I am asking Congress to pass the American Freedom Act. This will assure that we are free to speak our minds, and act upon our speech. But to be truly free, we must not tolerate those actions that strike at the heart of freedom: disagreement and dissent. These evils threaten our greatness; they divide rather than unite.

When we speak, we speak as one. When we act, we act as one.

Our schools, colleges and universities must be the bastion in our call to greatness. Students must know that the history of our great nation is one of compassion, loyalty, commitment to the American dream. We must always be strong; evil preys on the weak. We must not tolerate any instruction that seeks to detract from the history of America's greatness. In the past, we have banned such evil teachings as CRT and "Don't Say Gay," and this has made us a better, greater people.

Wayward businesses who dared to question America's greatness have learned that cooperation through support is far better than facing the consequences of their deviant actions.

Those who would undercut our greatness have also learned their lesson by the true American patriots who sued these evildoers in court to make them act like real Americans. We as your elected leaders know what is best for you and our cherished nation, and we know you will always be there with your unwavering support and absolute loyalty.

To those who continue to engage in protests and other acts of violence and dissent, your day is over. The words of our Declaration of Independence and Constitution were never meant to allow those thoughts and actions that threaten the very foundation of our government and our nation.

To those of you who believe the courts will provide a safe harbor for your bad behavior, I say this: we now have justices and judges who interpret the Constitution and laws of our great nation as they were written and intended at the time.

Our judiciary will not be a haven for your un-American conduct.

My fellow Americans and true patriots, you understand the price of freedom. You understand that we cannot, will not and must not tolerate any word or deed that calls into question the sacrifices you made to assure freedom, as well and liberty and justice, for you, your loved ones, and your fellow Americans.

Together, we will continue to expand our greatness. We will seek out and remove those who would strike a blow at the heart of our greatness.

In closing, I ask each of you to go forward and speak the words of liberty and justice for all who believe in the true greatness of our beloved country.

Welcome to our brave new world!

SUPREME COURT HYPOCRISY ON ABORTION

Today, author and historian Heather Cox Richardson exposes the rank hypocrisy of the right about abortion. The disclosure of the draft opinion by Justice Alito overruling Roe v. Wade has sent a shock wave through the nation.

Predictably, conservatives are outraged that this opinion was leaked; Democrats, moderate Republicans and independents and are outraged that a 50-year precedent has been tossed notwithstanding the fact that a significant majority of Americans support a woman's right to choose.

And make no mistake about it, this draft opinion is supported by four other justices, and it only takes five to declare what the Constitution means. Richardson calls out the three Trump justices, Gorsuch, Kavanaugh and Barrett– all of whom testified under oath during their confirmation hearing that Roe v. Wade was long-standing precedent and settled law. So much for testifying under oath and then acting contrary to that testimony.

But that's not the only source of unmitigated gall and blatant hypocrisy. In his draft opinion, Alito said in response to what the people want: "We cannot allow our decisions to be affected by extraneous influences such as concern about the public's reaction to our work." Imagine that! The justices don't care what the people think. Correction. The six conservative justices don't care what most Americans think. So, the logical question is who do these justices listen to? Richardson's answer: evangelicals and social conservatives; religious groups that had previously avoided politics.

Did these three justices lie under oath? Why are most of the justices supporting evangelicals and social conservatives, even though the vast majority of Americans oppose justices invoking their political views into their opinions?

Richardson notes that the Supreme Court has never taken away a constitutional right; this would be a first. And it won't be the last. On the right-wing agenda is much of the social justice/civil rights/voting rights laws covering the years since FDR's New Deal and the Warren Court years.

There certainly should be a complete and thorough investigation, but not the one the conservatives are clamoring for; investigate whether three justices lied to get their seats on the Court. Investigate what political and ideological influences are now at play at the highest court in our nation. Investigate the real pressing issues that most Americans really care about.

The leaked opinion affects the so-called integrity of the Court (although considering Justice Clarence Thomas's situation, whether he truly cares about the Court's integrity is an open question). That is not nearly as pressing as justices who might have gained their seats by subterfuge, or a Court insulated from the people, as if they sit in some ivory tower and discern the Constitution's meaning from divine providence. That's nonsense.

WHO RELEASED THE SUPREME COURT'S ABORTION DECISION? CONSPIRACIES ABOUND

This is the kind of stuff that feeds conspiracy theories. Just what we need, another conspiracy theory. The fact is one person's speculation is just as good as another's.

The conservatives stand to gain because it solidifies the core majority and might just bring along CJ Roberts, who's a stickler for the integrity of the Court, regardless of its diminishing aura.

The liberals stand to gain because it triggers protests now rather than during the heat of the summer. But protests tend to simmer down over time, and if they reach a peak earlier rather than later, it's hard to keep that momentum leading up to the November elections.

The contrary is people are going to protest no matter what, and they will protest as hard and if they believe it's necessary. The point of this is both sides stand to gain, and the only thing that suffers is the Court's image. After Clarence Thomas and his wife's Big Lie efforts, the Court's image is tanking anyway.

I saw a couple of articles quoting legal experts who say no crime has been committed, and any laws that might tangentially cover this call for not much more than a slap on the wrist.

I won't speculate because I really don't care; this is the Court's problem and there are ways to deal with it. As for jail time, how much time did Daniel Ellsberg serve for releasing confidential information about our government's handling of the Vietnam War, a matter far more profound than the early release of a Court opinion already agreed to by four other justices? The answer: none,

THE BACKLASH CONTINUES OVER THE PROSPECTIVE ABORTION DECISION; WE WERE WARNED

At the heart of the leaked Supreme Court decision overruling Roe v. Wade is the view that a woman's right to choose to have an abortion is not "deeply rooted in this Nation's history and tradition." What other rights that encased in previous Supreme Court decisions that are now at risk remain to be seen, but there is no doubt that others will be targeted.

Missing from Justice Samuel Alito's authoritarian missive is any recognition of individual rights that are "deeply rooted in this Nation's history and tradition."

The five freedoms of the First Amendment—speech, religion, press, assembly and petitioning for redress—would be meaningless without the right of association. Yet, the word "association" doesn't appear in the Bill of Rights.

Also missing is any cogent discussion of the various guarantees in the Constitution itself that create zones of privacy, which is at the heart of an individual's freedom to choose. The Third Amendment in its prohibition against the quartering of soldiers "in any house" in time of peace without the consent of the owner is another facet of that privacy. The Fourth Amendment explicitly affirms the "right of the people to be secure in their persons, houses, papers, and effects, against unreasonable searches and seizures." The Fifth Amendment, in its Self-Incrimination Clause, allows each citizen to create a zone of privacy which government may not force him/her to surrender to his/her detriment. The Ninth Amendment provides: "The enumeration in the Constitution, of certain rights, shall not be construed to deny or disparage others retained by the people."

This is a decision that classically demonstrates the end justifies the means. The right-leaning justices knew they wanted certain rights overruled; all they needed was some rationale, however fashioned, to support their conclusion. They knew the true believers would buy it whole hog; they also knew the rest would find it a gift to the extreme right.

In her column today, historian and author Heather Cox Richardson clearly identifies the source of this tectonic shift away from the protection of individual rights: religion, specifically according to Washington Post columnist Jennifer Rubin, "a religious tyranny....in which the right seeks to ... establish a society that aligns with a minority view of America as a White, Christian country."

It's not as if we haven't been warned that this would happen here. In his 2005 book "American Theocracy," American author and political commentator Kevin Phillips contends that religion is, by far, the most accurate predictor of political and ideological belief. He cites this as the primary determinant of who picked what side during what he refers to as the three great civil wars between English speaking people: the English Civil War in the 17th century, the American Revolution, and the American Civil War.

He notes that, at the time of publication, 40 percent of the Republican coalition is made up of such voters. Phillips cites to quotes by former President George W. Bush suggesting that he is speaking for God, and points to past leaders, such as Roman Dictator Julius Caesar who made similar statements. (We hear similar views expressed by former President Trump and his supporters.) Phillips points to hostility by the social conservatives towards science in general, and Darwinian evolution in particular, but particularly focuses on the end-times prophecies of what he refers to as Christian Reconstructionists.

Phillips traces the history of American religion. He argues that the pilgrims who emigrated to the New World before the American Revolution were religious outsiders, who were non-conformist and more radical than the establishment would allow (which was why they left Europe in the first place). He points to a history of highly emotional religious practices in the 17th and 18th centuries. He then argues that after "fundamentalist religion" (particularly Evangelical and the newly formed Pentecostal branches) were set back after the Scopes Monkey Trial, they appeared to have been dealt a permanent blow.

Phillips cites statistical studies that suggest that after this point, fundamentalist religion grew at a rapid rate, while mainstream denominations declined (this was covered to most observers at the time due to other circumstances, such as the increase in population at the time.)

Meanwhile, barricades have been placed around the Supreme Court, and Justice Alito has cancelled appointments.

BASEBALL MEMORIES FROM MY CHILDHOOD

As a kid growing up in the Bronx, I went to many games in the old Yankee Stadium and Polo Grounds. I got to see Whitey Ford, Mickey Mantle, and Yogi Berra; Willie Mays and Duke Snider and Roy Campanella. I also got to see Bob Feller when the former Cleveland Indians came to town.

I remember the great debate in New York in the 1950s over who was the best centerfielder, Mantle, Mays, or Snider. Each fan chose the player whose team he rooted for. For me, it was Mantle. But over the years, as I became more familiar with the sport, I felt that overall, it was Mays; for sheer power, it was Mantle; and for sheer aggressiveness particularly in the field, it was Snider.

True story. I was an elementary school hall monitor who, with others and as a reward, went to a Yankee game against the Tigers in May 1955. The Yankees won 5-3 and the game wasn't particularly remarkable except for one thing: it was the only time in his great career that Mickey Mantle hit three homers in one game. Drove in all five runs, too. I had the game ticket but lost it moving to Florida. Another true story. My dad wanted to take my brother and me to a Dodgers game at Ebbets Field. I had never been there (and never did get to see it) but the Yankees were playing Baltimore and I insisted on seeing my beloved Yankees. My dad relented. Well, the Baltimore pitcher took a no-hitter into the ninth inning before the Yankees managed one hit. I was excited that I almost saw a no-hitter--until on the way home, we heard over the radio that Carl Erskine pitched a no-hitter. Needless to say, I wasn't a happy camper.

There is nothing like childhood memories.

A TOXIC MIX: IGNORANCE AND STUPIDITY

James Lankford is a 54-year-old junior senator from Oklahoma. He is currently in his second term. He's on record as saying the current version of the Republican Party is unquestionably "the party of Lincoln." That's right, he believes today's right wing-dominated party is still the party of Abraham Lincoln.

Ignorance is defined as a lack of knowledge or information.

Stupidity is defined as behavior that shows a lack of good sense or judgment.

Here we have a middle-aged member of what has been called the greatest deliberative body in world history telling his audience that the takeover of the Republican Party by the extreme right is simply following in the footsteps of

Abraham Lincoln, the president credited with freeing the slaves and saving the union.

Captured by the religious right, the Republican Party is undertaking an all-out assault on personal freedoms and liberty, first eliminating the right of a woman to choose to have an abortion, but certainly not stopping there. Other reproductive rights, and well as civil rights and liberties that were achieved through blood and battle, are targeted for extinction as well.

Yet, there are those who confidently assert that Lincoln would approve, since today's Republican Party is his Republican Party.

Back to those two definitions. I don't know whether Sen. Lankford is simply trying to give his audience a confidence boost by filling them with this line, or whether he truly believes it. And I don't know whether his audience believes that they represent the party of Lincoln.

But what is obvious from the face of this statement is that it shows ignorance of American history and stupidity in saying it to convince others to believe it to be true.

It most certainly is not. Lankford either knows nothing of the history of party realignment and is just passing along his ignorance to his audience, or he knows he's not being truthful and simply wants to give his audience a false sense of confidence by lying to them.

So, Sen. Lankford is either ignorant of history, or shows a lack of good sense and judgment—in other words, stupid.

For the benefit of Sen. Lankford and those who believe his claptrap, here is a link that discusses the history of party realignment in America. It's a simple, relatively short article that captures this history. It shouldn't take very long to become educated on this subject.

Any time you hear anyone–most especially an elected or appointed public official—make this asinine statement, please inform of this bit of history. History is, after all, a wonderful teacher.

In the 21st century, we should expect our government leaders to be educated and informed. Sadly, some fall through the crack. Too many. And we are witnessing the results of ignorance and stupidity daily from those entrusted with the well-being of our nation and ourselves.

WHEN PIGS FLY

Scrolling down Facebook, I invariably see posts asking for my signature supporting a national voting rights law, a law legalizing abortion nationwide, or a law taking the state legislature out of setting education policy, among other issues.

I also see ads seeking contributions for Democratic candidates who promise to protect individual rights from the authoritarians.

Asking the current Congress to pass any of these laws is a waste of time. As the saying goes, these laws will pass this Congress–or any Congress that the Republicans control or unduly influence–the day pigs fly.

As for candidate posts, I don't see any for Republican candidates. I presume they have enough donations from corporate contributors and their base that they don't have to use Facebook to solicit funds.

But are the Democrats so hard up for money that they need to use Facebook, and perhaps other social media, to raise funds? Where are the big Democratic donors, and the party's own base? Are these candidates not receiving sufficient support from their own party faithful?

We know what the Republicans intend to do once they have control of Congress next year, and then the White House two years thereafter. They have been unabashed about how they will structure the government from the far right. Presumably, in the face of Republican arrogance and hubris, the tens of millions that call themselves Democrats who are revulsed at what the Republicans are doing, and planning to do, would be funding their candidates big-time. Apparently, this isn't happening. One can only wonder why.

These ads purport to show the Republican candidate running one or two percentage points ahead of the Democratic candidate. Whether this is an accurate poll number, or a teaser to show how close the races are and how additional funding can turn the numbers around, is worthy of consideration.

The ads I see are usually for Val Demings, Stacey Abrams, and Raphael Warnock. I suppose, but don't know for sure, that other Facebook pages have similar ads for other Democratic candidates. And perhaps for a few Republican candidates as well, although considering the status of redistricting and reapportionment efforts, they don't need to push nearly as hard as the Democrats.

It seems that criticism of Republicans has the same effect on them as water off a duck's back. Even the demonstrations against the Supreme Court's putative abortion decision, while it has aroused passions across the nation, don't seem to affect Republican officeholders. At least, not yet.

There is a psychological principle that people become desensitized when continuously bombarded by outrageous words and actions. In short, when outrage meets overexposure, anger becomes "so what?"

I fear this is what is happening, and it is a dangerous tipping point.

The Democrats are no doubt hoping that the Congressional committee's public hearings on the assault on the capital last year will resonate and energize Democratic voters. Perhaps criminal indictments will also serve that purpose. But whether Democratic anger, resentment, commitment to reverse the course we're now on will remain intense enough over the summer and into the November elections is an unanswered question. And the Democrats, faced with a flagging economy and an unpopular president at this moment, would make a big mistake putting all their eggs into this anger basket.

They need to take charge of the message. As the party in power, they should be out there delivering that message every day in strong, unmistakable terms. As California Gov. Gavin Newsom said, "where the hell is my party?" Weak, tepid responses won't cut it.

The party is not being seen or heard.

And time is a fleeting.

FEAR, GALL, NO SURPRISE, UNABASHED HYPOCRISY, AND NAIVETE

FEAR–Fear has been the constant motivator throughout history. Fear of communists (Joseph McCarthy) and that recurring bogeyman, socialism. This one goes back to the days of FDR, Truman, JFK, LBJ and any Democrat who supports programs designed to help the many among us. By labeling these efforts as socialism, the fear factor works. Try telling the right that there isn't a single country in the world that is socialist. They deny that simply because they believe the opposite is so, facts be damned. The Baltic countries that have a mix of socialist elements as well as capitalist elements are among the happiest in the world. Having been to the Netherlands, Denmark, Sweden, Finland, Norway, etc., and seen how people live there, I can attest to their happiness. Why people support those who generate the most fear is something for the psychologists and perhaps psychiatrists.

GALL–Supreme Court Justice Clarence Thomas has expressed concern over declining respect for our institutions, the judiciary in particular. Considering his major contribution to this decline, leading to the ongoing ethics investigation into his connection to his wife's actions before and during the January 6, 2021 attack on the capital, he is the recipient of today's Unmitigated Gall award (if only there were one.).

NO SURPRISE—Florida Gov. Ron DeSantis promised he would get a favorable result for his restrictive voting laws that a federal district judge declared unconstitutional. He was right. The 11th Circuit Court of Appeals reinstated his draconian laws. That should not be a surprise, considering most of the judges are Republican appointees. But, of course, we all know judges and justices are independent thinkers, beholden to no political party, and their decisions are not driven by politics. Uh huh.

UNABASHED HYPOCRISY–Sens. Mitch McConnell and John Kennedy, among others on the right, are incensed and outraged over the brazen lawlessness surrounding the release of the draft Supreme Court decision overruling Roe v. Wade. Strange that they express no outrage over efforts by their fellow legislators to aid and abet the insurrection at the Capital last year, or the repeated lies and aberrant conduct by Trump and his eager Congressional followers. A little hypocrisy here? Actually, a lot of brazen, unabashed hypocrisy.

NAIVETE–Sen. Susan Collins is either the most simple-minded or naive member of Congress. Look at her latest statement, this one about Justices Gorsuch and Kavanaugh. Doesn't she know that nominees will say what they want to gain confirmation? She has been in the Senate 26 years. Hasn't she learned anything about politics? This is the same senator who said, after Donald Trump's first impeachment, that he learned his lesson. Yeah, right. What's next senator, that the Senate will vigorously investigate the January 6 assault on the capital because Mitch McConnell privately told you he would after the November 2022 election? If you believe that, there is some oceanfront property available in Omaha that you can get for a great price!

ABORTION RIGHTS DISCONNECT, AND A WARNING

As the current right-leaning Supreme Court stands on the precipice of overruling Roe v. Wade, which gives women the right to choose to have an abortion under its terms, there are several vital factors that come into play.

We know that five of the six conservative justices have already gone on record as opposing Roe v. Wade despite broad public support for a woman' right to choose.

Gallup polls show Americans' support for abortion in all or most cases at 80% in May 2021, only slightly higher than in 1975 (76%).

The share of Americans in Gallup's poll who say abortion is morally acceptable reached a record high of 47% in May, up from a low of 36% in 2009, and a Quinnipiac poll found support for abortion being legal in all or most cases reached a near-record high in September with 63% support.

Support for the Supreme Court's abortion precedent in Roe v. Wade is similar, with a November Quinnipiac poll finding that 63% agree with the court's ruling; and 72% of respondents in a January Marquette Law School poll and 69% of January CNN poll respondents oppose it being overturned.

A January CNN poll found a 59% majority want their state to have laws that are "more permissive than restrictive" on abortion if Roe goes away, while only 20% want their state to ban abortion entirely (another 20% want it to be restricted but not banned).

An Associated Press/NORC poll in June found 87% support abortion when the woman's life is in danger, 84% support exceptions in the case of rape or incest, and 74% support abortion if the child would be born with a life-threatening illness.

Significantly, all religious groups support a woman's right to choose, except Evangelicals.

This is where the disconnect comes into play. Sen. Mitch McConnell, who stands to become senate majority leader once again should the Republicans attain a majority in the senate, has gone on record saying a national law banning abortions is possible.

Read that last sentence again. Despite broad support for a woman's right to choose, McConnell says the senate is listening not to the majority, but to the Evangelicals.

The Democrats have voiced support for a national woman's right to choose law, but don't have the votes to pass it, even though they have slim majorities in both houses of Congress. In any event, all the party's leaders are doing is ranting and raving, expressing moral outrage.

The Democrat's support for a national law, however, has given the Republicans an idea. Thanks to McConnell, we now know precisely what their plan is once they gain majority control of both houses.

Of course, a national abortion ban law won't be possible so long as President Biden has the veto power. But should a Donald Trump, Ron DeSantis or Greg Abbott, or any other far right-wing official gain the White House in 2024, there will be nothing standing in the way of a total national ban on abortions, regardless of reasons.

But why would an empowered Republican right-wing stop there?

We see what Republican governors have done in many of our states; why not follow their lead?

Here is the warning.

With complete control over both branches of the federal government, and a genuflective judiciary headed by a staunchly conservative Supreme Court, envision if you will the following:

A national ban on teaching Critical Race Theory (or anything that smacks of teaching about slavery as it really was; or the adoption of any law that effectively re-writes history to reflect the conservative point of view), A national "Don't Say Gay" law, A national election law creating a police force enforcing restrictive voting laws targeting certain groups of voters, A national thought and speech control law for college and university campuses, A national open-carry or constitutional carry gun law with no permitting, licensing or training requirements, A national law allowing citizens to sue fellow citizens for daring to offend, causing hurt feelings or psychological discomfort.

And on and on. What additional national laws would be passed–all in the name of freedom, liberty, and justice?

Think it can't happen? That's the wrong question. It's happening; just read McConnell's statement. The real question is what is being done to counter what they have planned for our country'?

REALITY CHECK TIME: THE JUDICIARY AND OTHER ITEMS ON THE DEMOCRAT WISH LIST

Reality check time. First reality check: Justices are appointed and confirmed just like every other presidential appointee that requires Senate confirmation. It is a political process, and we need to avoid pretending that somehow the same process that is used for cabinet officers, etc., will result in a judiciary that is independent of politics. What we're facing with the current judiciary is nothing new; FDR had his battles with the Supreme Court almost 100 years ago. over ideological differences.

Presidents are not going to appoint justices and judges based on a disagreement over burning issues of the day. Occasionally, a president makes a mistake: Eisenhower with Earl Warren being the most classic. There have been others.

But since the nomination of Robert Bork, the process has become overtly political....and that's not going to change, at least for the foreseeable future. We can expect conservative presidents to nominate conservative justices and judges and a conservative senate to confirm. And vice versa. The only possible way you'll get moderates is if either the president or senate is run by the other party.

Second reality check: all those ads on Facebook about supporting legislation taking Roe v. Wade nationwide are wasted efforts. It's not going to happen if the Republicans hold sway over both houses of Congress, or even one house. Same for all the other things the left wants, like term limits for justices and judges. Not going to happen. Focus all energies on electing Democrats to office–and not the Manchin and Sinema kind of paper Democrats. Choose Democratic candidates committed to all these issues you want to become law, but you know in your heart of hearts won't happen under the current state of affairs.

Work hard to introduce them to the public through a mass education program. Point out in no uncertain terms what the opposition stands for, and what they will do if elected. Paint it dark, draconian, and dystopian because it is. Contrast that with what precisely the Democrats will do. Be as bold and brazen as the opposition is. Develop a get-out-the-vote plan that does the job. And on election day, leave no stone unturned in getting Democrat voters to the polls.

THE DEMOCRATS MUST STOP ACTING LIKE THE KEYSTONE KOPS

Typically, when the Republicans unleash their latest right-wing blast, the Democrats react by raising their arms in disgust, running in circles, ranting and raving at how terrible this is, only to return to their position to await the next madness.

Their reaction reminds me of the fabled Keystone Kops. For those who don't recall these madcap merry men of yore, the Keystone Cops (often spelled "Keystone Kops") are fictional, humorously incompetent policemen featured in silent film slapstick comedies produced by Mack Sennett for his Keystone Film Company between 1912 and 1917.

They could be seen in constant motion, meeting each predicament in a predictable manner: raising their arms, frantically running in circles, frequently bumping into one another, accomplishing nothing.

Wikipedia notes that Keystone Kops "has been used to criticize any group for its mistakes and lack of coordination, particularly if either trait was exhibited after a great deal of energy and activity. For example, in criticizing the Department of Homeland Security's response to Hurricane Katrina, Senator Joseph Lieberman claimed that emergency workers under DHS chief Michael Chertoff 'ran around like Keystone Kops, uncertain about what they were supposed to do or uncertain how to do it.'"

This is an apt description of the Democrats' response to anything from the right wing; whether it be their reaction to the leaked Supreme Court abortion decision, voting restrictions, "Don't Say Gay" and anti-Critical Race Theory" laws, curtailment of academic freedom, etc. The subject doesn't matter; the reaction is the same. Lots of activity full of sound and fury, signifying nothing.

As the Democrats scurry around venting their disgust, there is one thing that they aren't doing: energizing their voters. As President Biden talks up infrastructure, voters are concerned more with rising gas prices and the cost of living, and a war between Russia and Ukraine. Passing an infrastructure bill is important, but it's also yesterday's news. It's hard to feel good about a new bridge when you can barely pay your bills—if in fact you can pay your bills.

The Democrats need to stop acting like Keystone Kops. They need to forge a clear, coherent message that is substantive, timely and meaningful. And they need to do it yesterday.

IN RICK SCOTT'S UPSIDE-DOWN WORLD, DONALD TRUMP IS COMPETENCE PERSONIFIED, WHILE JOE BIDEN IS INCOMPETENT

Florida Republican Sen. Rick Scott has gone on record saying what conservative media outlets have been harping on for some time now. Here is his statement:

"Let's be honest here. Joe Biden is unwell. He's unfit for office. He's incoherent, incapacitated and confused. He doesn't know where he is half the time. He's incapable of leading and he's incapable of carrying out his duties. Period. Everyone knows it. No one is willing to say it. But we have to, for the sake of the country. Joe Biden can't do the job."

He could have said the same thing about Donald Trump, and considering Trump's record, it would have been on target; but to the right-wing that would be heresy. During his four years as president, Trump was known for his gaffes, lies, inane comments, and downright stupidity, such as when he famously said bleach could be ingested to fight off COVID.

(Here is a link to 50 of his famous gaffes: there are so many more. https://www.theatlantic.com/unthinkable/)

But to Scott, Donald Trump epitomizes competent leadership. After all, it was Scott who gave Trump the National Republican Senatorial Committee's (NRSC) Champion of Freedom award because he "worked hard." Sure, he worked hard, but at what? We know the answer: cozying up to Putin and other dictators while criticizing our NATO allies. Specifically, and most profoundly, he criticized the democratically elected Ukraine president Volodymyr Zelensky, while supporting Russian dictator and warmonger Putin.

You will recall it was Trump's call to Zelensky that led to Trump's first impeachment. Congress appropriated funds for Ukraine, but Trump held up sending those funds in return for a promise from Zelensky to gather evidence–dirt on Joe Biden's son, Hunter–to use against Biden in the 2020 presidential campaign. Considering this, it's no wonder Trump opposes Zelensky and supports Putin.

Scott also voted against the creation of the committee investigating the January 6 attack on the capital. No need to wonder why; we know. It's the same reason Trump has avoided being deposed under oath; the same reason he's stonewalled every investigation into his conduct and activities over the years: he has something to hide. Lots of things to hide.

Now, Trump is trying to recruit Scott for Senate majority leader. Let's see, what is the phrase that applies to a favor or advantage granted or expected in return for something? It's called quid pro quo. Say nice things about Trump, even give him an award and block any investigation that puts him at risk, and he will see that you get something in return, like Senate majority leader. See any quid pro quo here?

Be careful Rick; remember that, with Trump, loyalty is a one-way street. Better not say or do anything that upsets his sensibilities, or you will find yourself on the outs, like so many others who have genuflected before him, only to regain some measure of dignity and disagree with him. But for He Who Must Not be Disobeyed, disagreement is an act of treason. Of course, to expect Scott to challenge Trump is expecting too much.

Oh, and by the way, senator, 81 million people found Biden more competent as president than your master.

RELIGION, THE FIRST AMENDMENT AND FREEDOM OF CHOICE

There can be no doubt that religion has played a vital role in world history. Just visit the many houses of worship in other countries and you will see firsthand the power, force and influence religion has had down through the ages.

It has been said that religion serves several societal functions. These include (a) giving meaning and purpose to life, (b) reinforcing social unity and stability, (c) serving as an agent of social control of behavior, (d) promoting physical and psychological well-being, and (e) motivating people to work for positive social change. Religion speaks to a higher purpose and accountability to a higher being.

Religion is such a powerful influence that it has been said more people have died over religious causes than any other single cause for war. This appears not to be true, however. Wikipedia notes that according to the Encyclopedia of Wars, out of all 1,763 known/recorded historical conflicts, 121, or 6.87%, had religion as their primary cause. Matthew White's The Great Big Book of Horrible Things gives religion as the primary cause of 11 of the world's 100 deadliest atrocities. This, of course, refers to religion as the primary cause; it doesn't mean that religion wasn't at least somewhat involved in other wars.

There are many different religions, each interpreting these five functions differently. I was surprised to learn that there are over 4,000 recognized religions in the world. This may surprise you as well. These religions consist of churches, congregations, faith groups, tribes, cultures, and movements. The 12 most influential religions are: Christianity, Islam, Hindu, Buddhism, Sikhism, Judaism, Baha'i, Confucianism, Jainism, Taoism, and Zoroastrianism. As of 2020, Christianity (2.3 billion adherents), Islam (1.9 billion) and Hindu (1.1 billion) make up over 70% of all religious adherents in the world.

Problems arise, however, when one religion presumes superiority over others, or when one group condemns a religion as the source of all evil. The former instills fear in other believers that they face persecution, or worse, for practicing their faith. The latter is no more graphically demonstrated that Hitler's Germany.

The madness of Hitler, and the state of permanent tension between Israel and some of the Arab countries aside, religions bring awareness to the significant differences in belief and practice. In searching for a richer and deeper understanding of diverse cultures, it is incumbent on all of us to embrace religious tolerance, understanding, acceptance and a willingness to move beyond our differences.

This brings us to our First Amendment's freedom of religion guarantee.

The first amendment to the U.S. Constitution states, "Congress shall make no law respecting an establishment of religion or prohibiting the free exercise thereof." The two parts are known as the "establishment clause" and the "free exercise clause" respectively.

Thomas Jefferson referred to this language as creating a wall of separation between church and state. But what precisely does this mean? This constitutional language has been the subject of differing interpretations by the Supreme Court over the years.

Generally, the First Amendment ensures both that the government does not show preference to a certain religion and that the government does not take away an individual's ability to exercise religion. In other words, the church should not rule over the state, and the state cannot rule over the church. Religion is too important to be a government program or a political pageant. Everyone in the United States has the right to practice his or her own religion, or no religion at all.

Today, the establishment clause prohibits all levels of government from either advancing or inhibiting religion. **The establishment clause separates church from state, but not religion from politics or public life. Individual citizens are free to bring their religious convictions into the public arena**. And the constitutional right of people to petition and assemble assure that individual convictions can and do become group convictions. But **the government**

is prohibited from favoring one religious view over another or even favoring religion over non-religion.

The highlighted language above gets to the nub of where we are today. No subject more reflects the debate over these First Amendment clauses than abortion, framed as either freedom of a woman to choose by the left, or baby killing on the right.

If people are free to bring their religious beliefs into the public arena, the natural tendency is to have those beliefs take prominence over others, and ultimately codified into law that governs everyone, including those with different beliefs. This is no different than supporting or opposing any program or idea; the ultimate goal of any lobbying effort is to gain acceptance and having it adopted into law, or having an existing law defeated or overruled.

We know that there are strong religious overtones driving this debate, but here is the quintessential question that this burning issue raises:

Doesn't a decision by the government involve favoring one religious group over another? We know the Evangelicals oppose abortion under all circumstances. Whatever happened to the adage "live and let live;" that is, we should tolerate the opinions and behavior of others so that they will similarly tolerate your own?

Some pundits have legitimately expressed concern that we are becoming a theocracy, where one religion's doctrine dominates others. Author and historian Heather Cox Richardson writes frequently about this point. Author and commentator Kevin Phillips has written extensively about this in his book "American Theocracy."

Recall the First Amendment's jurisprudence that bans the government from showing preference for one religion or advancing thc cause of one religion over another. Should this hot-button issue—including birth control–be left out of our national debate; that is, simply let the people make their own decisions for themselves, without religion or government involvement? Live and let live?

If the infusion of religion into government is constitutionally permissible, how far does this infusion extend? In short, after abortion and birth control, what's next? Same-sex marriage? Interracial marriage? And what religion-infused issues lie beyond these?

And the debate rages.

"THE ONLY THING WE HAVE TO FEAR IS FEAR ITSELF."

FDR said this in the context of the worst economic depression in this country's history. After World War I, the dominant economic model was one of laissez faire; a leave business alone approach. Recall Calvin Coolidge's statement "the business of America is business."

Unbridled capitalism brought about the Great Depression. In the popular account the stock market went wild in the late 1920s, with people gambling recklessly on stocks and shares, often with money they didn't have. Shares could only go up, they thought, but they were wrong. When the market crashed in 1929, Hoover had no plan to deal with this existential crisis. He kept saying "prosperity is just around the corner." That is not a plan.

Roosevelt knew the only plan to save the country was government involvement priming the economic pump. Predictably, he was blasted by the conservatives as a socialist. But where was the Republicans' plan? Hoover took the insanity approach, doing the same thing over and over again, expecting a different result. Remember his "two chickens in every pot" promise to the American people as the economy began tanking? All words, no plan. The New Deal itself didn't end the Great Depression; World War II did. (As an aside, it was the conservative Republican isolationists that prepared for World War II that much more difficult by opposing any aid to Great Britain earlier than Lend-Lease, which gave Hitler the one thing he needed in the late 1930s–time.)

But how many more lives would have been lost, how much more suffering would we have endured, if not for FDR's New Deal? History repeats itself. Today, any Democrat president is branded as a socialist if he offers programs designed to benefit the majority. So long as big business gets its corporate welfare in the form of tax benefits and other legislative gifts not available to the general population, not to mention legislation that appeases the Evangelicals, the Republicans have no problem.

But how many of those who blame the liberals today for these "socialist" programs are themselves recipients of social security, workers' compensation, unemployment compensation, and other programs that provide a lifeline when things go south? What about the benefits Congress approves for themselves? History is clear that the conservatives' greatest problem is their inability to govern. Oh, they can rant until they foam at the mouth about radical leftist, socialists, communists, etc. But which party is now cozying up to Putin, the most dangerous despot on the planet? Not the Democrats.

The party that claims the high ground on freedom and liberty is diminishing both every day. What we are reaping today is a result of four years of a clueless, inept president treated like a deity by his groveling enablers and mindless supporters. The one thing they do better than the Democrats is lie and gaslight. Biden was handed this biggest government mess since FDR. Sure, I'm concerned whether a 79-year-old man can handle the stress of the job, but in the context of what the alternative was, I'll take him.

FEARMONGERING AND RISING GAS PRICES

Fearmongering lies at the heart of the Republican playbook. Regardless of the Democrat proposals, the right wing typically responds by calling them radical, socialist, etc. Of course, the Republicans have no plan of their own, and refuse to work with the Democrats on any programs designed to help the average American. Gas prices are soaring, but so are big oil profits.

The Biden Administration is releasing 180 million barrels of oil over six months from our Strategic Petroleum Reserves. Biden has asked Congress to do its part by making oil companies pay fees on wells from their leases that they haven't used in years, and on acres of public lands that they are hoarding without producing. Biden is also asking the oil companies to do their part by not sitting idly by and reaping huge profits; they have lowered prices during past energy crises, and they could do so again.

Fat chance for the Republicans to do anything to actually deal with a nationwide crisis. They believe they're better off just screaming and yelling at what's not being done, hoping the voters don't wake up and realize how complicit they are in making sure nothing gets done that might adversely affect the oil companies' bottom line.

Fat chance the oil companies will take any action that might just affect their unprecedented profits. What does the right wing expect the Biden Administration to do, set gas prices? The Republicans would foam at the mouth at such a suggestion. The Republican Party simply doesn't believe in governing; they are spending their time and energies pandering to their voters, hoping they won't ask their own party what it's doing to deal with this crisis.

COMMUNISM ON CAMPUS: A CASE OF DEFLECTION FROM THE REAL FEAR

Recently, Florida Gov. Ron DeSantis signed into law a measure aimed at ensuring that public school students learn about "the evils of communism." At his press conference announcing his signing, DeSantis spent part of his comments criticizing what he contends is a rise in communist sympathies on college and university campuses.

But it's what he didn't include in his legislation and message that should be of real concern: the evils of fascism. He made no mention of the rise of authoritarianism in America, or the lessons learned from relatively recent history that the fear of communism is a strawman, an attempt to deflect from the very real fear of fascism in America. This legislation, and his comments about it, recall the "red scare" days Joe McCarthy in the 1950s. What's next; a list of "known communist" on college and university campuses? How about the state department? The entertainment industry? Are we to go back to the sad, embarrassing days of phony "known communist sympathizers" and blacklists?

From "anti-Woke" legislation to intellectual freedom surveys on college and university campuses, the trend is unmistakable: although passed in the name of freedom, these laws are part of a concerted attack on academic freedom while legitimizing right wing extremism.

These laws, and others like them, assume that dangerous liberal thinking is running rampant in our schools and institutions of higher learning, and, as a result, the conservative viewpoint must be given equal access. This is bunk. If equal access were the goal, the works of William F. Buckley, Jr., Barry Goldwater, and George Will would be required reading, as well as other works of rational conservative thinkers. Conservative speakers who adhere to traditional principles would appear to present their positions. In any event, attempts at a level playing field would not require legislation that shuts off dialogue, debate, and knowledge.

What is really being sought here is an effort to equate gaining knowledge through study and debate on issues of public importance with the unhinged rhetoric of a Marjorie Taylor Greene, Matt Gaetz, Jim Jordan, Paul Gosar, or any of their ilk. Make no mistake about it, the Republican party is intent on adding more of these extremists to Congress in this year's election cycle. The party leaders will do everything they can to engender enough fear and hatred in the voting populace to accomplish their goal. It's not a stretch to add communists to their wild rants about radical leftist extremists, socialists…we know the rest; we hear it every day from the extreme right.

This effort at legitimizing their lunacy should make it abundantly clear the road the Republican Party wants America to travel.

Over the past five years or so, we have witnessed the far right's demonization of vulnerable and marginalized groups; repeated attacks on the free press as "the enemy of the people;" the constant undermining of facts, knowledge, science and expertise; incessant spreading of disinformation; politicizing law enforcement, the courts and the military; restricting voting rights and expanding executive power.

This is straight out of the fascist playbook.

This extreme legislation is an example of thought control, banning the teaching of critical race theory (whatever it means as determined by the censors), imposing "Don't Say Gay" and eliminating the teaching of virtually any subject that makes one feel psychologically uncomfortable. This type of legislation, passed in the name of freedom and liberty, in fact does just the opposite by closing off avenues of teaching and learning. Teaching the history of the McCarthy era and communist witch hunts is itself subject to being blacklisted because it might cause psychological distress. It is legitimate to ask what other academic subjects will face the ax in the right wing's curriculum cleansing program. They know history repeats itself; but if history isn't taught, it follows that people won't know what evils to avoid.

Where is DeSantis when a Greene, Gaetz, Jordan, Gosar, etc., make outlandish statements, or issue promises or threats of what they and their kind will do once they gain control of Congress?

He's busy fighting against a non-existent communist bogeyman while his silence gives aid and comfort to those who represent the real threat to democracy.

SILENCING DISSENT

This was predictable. The right wing wouldn't be satisfied with its assault on academic freedom and its efforts at curriculum cleansing. The extremists must also silence all criticism of those who are hellbent on waging a culture war on constitutional rights and civil liberties.

This is the story about a Florida middle school principal who posted on Facebook her disagreement with the cleverly labelled Parental Rights in Education and Stop WOKE laws banning the teachings of critical race theory and discussion of sexual identity before the fourth grade. Never mind that neither is taught in public schools; the point here is that there must be no criticism of Gov. Ron DeSantis or the Florida legislature for passing and enforcing these draconian thought control laws.

This principal was outed by the social media police force that has arisen from this legislation. Citizen ratting on citizen–how American is that!

Also predictable is a right-wing legislator calling for the firing of this principal for daring to express her opinion on these laws.

He says he is all for free speech, but notes that there are consequences for speaking one's mind. And the consequence here is termination for expressing an opinion. Digest that last sentence. According to him–and his fellow right wingers–you are free to speak your mind only if you agree with what government is doing. Criticism of government action subjects you to punishment.

Someone needs to tell him and his kind that speech is not free if it can only be uttered in support of whatever government does. In America, we are free to engage in debate, criticize and even condemn government action, so long as what is said doesn't create a clear and present danger of violent actions. What this elected public official is advocating is silencing dissent–precisely what a fascist government does.

First Amendment's jurisprudence makes it very clear that robust debate on public issues of great importance lies at the heart of the right to free speech. Unless the judiciary ultimately decides that current jurisprudence on civil rights and academic freedom is wrong–the ramifications of which should be self-evident–the First Amendment's freedom of speech clause will protect this middle school principal.

But don't put it past the radical right wing to conjure up a way of assuring that people don't think. One way is to use soothing words like parental rights, or Florida freedom, in describing laws. That makes the masses feel good, so they just instinctively nod their heads in approval, mindlessly voice their support, and genuflect before their exalted leaders. That's how you control thought and action.

Pay attention to these words from Martin Niemoller:

"First they came for the socialists, and I did not speak out— because I was not a socialist.

Then they came for the trade unionists, and I did not speak out— because I was not a trade unionist.

Then they came for the Jews, and I did not speak out— because I was not a Jew.

Then they came for me—and there was no one left to speak for me."

TODAY'S SILENT MAJORITY MUST NOT REMAIN SILENT

In 1969, President Richard Nixon sought support for his plan to end the Vietnam War. During a televised speech, he uttered a phrase that was to characterize his years in office, until Watergate compelled his resignation. This is what he said:

"So tonight, to you, **the great silent majority of my fellow Americans**, I ask for your support. I pledged in my campaign for the Presidency to end the war in a way that we could win the peace. I have initiated a plan of action which will enable me to keep that pledge. The more support I can have from the American people, the sooner that pledge can be redeemed. For the more divided we are at home, the less likely the enemy is to negotiate in Paris. Let us be united for peace. Let us also be united against defeat. Because let us understand: North Vietnam cannot defeat or humiliate the United States. Only Americans can do that..."

Polls taken after his speech indicated that a "silent majority" sided with Nixon. The day after the speech, as supportive telegrams and letters streamed into the White House, an administration official clarified Nixon's concept of "silent majority": a "large and normally undemonstrative cross section of the country that until last night refrained from articulating its opinions on the war." (Quote from the New York Times, November 5, 1969.).

What Nixon did was presume the existence of a silent majority that supported his views; all he needed was some evidence of that support. Those telegrams and letters served his purpose. His use of television was most successful, even if his Vietnamization plan ultimately failed.

Why is this important today? Because just as Nixon cultivated a message that resonated with the silent majority, so is it necessary for those who speak for today's silent majority to craft a message that resonates with them.

It is estimated that about 30% of Americans are authoritarians who lean towards extreme conservatism, white supremacism, and other right-wing to far-right ideologies, paired with conspiratorial rhetoric alongside reactionary aspirations. (Interestingly, a smaller percentage, estimated at about 10%, support fascist principles, leading to the conclusion that a large number aren't aware of the relationship between authoritarianism and fascism.)

This means a substantial majority of Americans oppose right wing authoritarianism, regardless of its form.

Sadly, it's difficult to discern this from today's political discourse and current state of affairs. Considering the press play the Republican Party's far right extremists attract, it's not a stretch of the imagination for many to believe the far right's influence is greater than it really is. It's not, but as California Gov. Gavin Newsom said recently after the Supreme Court's abortion decision was leaked "where is (the Democrat) Party?" In short, he was asking: Where is the outrage? Where is the party leadership when America needs it to confront right wing radicalism?

After the horrific mass shooting by an avowed teenage racist that took the lives of 10 people at a Buffalo supermarket, the question asked yet again is why aren't the Democrat leaders calling out the radical right rhetoric, the poison that fuels this hatred? How many more hate crimes will it take for our informed and rational leaders to draw out the silent majority and say, "Enough is enough!"

Those in charge of our national security are unanimous in declaring that our greatest danger lies in domestic terrorism. Violent rhetoric and threats from the right are becoming normalized in everyday politics. What is being done to counteract this?

After each racially or ethnically motivated mass shooting, we hear calls for unity. Clearly, these calls aren't working. Getting meaningful legislation passed is a lost cause. Why aren't the Democrat leaders and their supporters, as well as independents and rational Republicans, crafting a message that will resonate with, and mobilize, the silent majority?

There are the usual calls for "sensible gun regulations," but that hasn't worked. The latest call is for social media to shut down all extreme right-wing sites, the kind this teenage mass killer followed. There are concerns about where you draw the line, but like a Supreme Court justice said about pornography: "I know it when I see it." Perhaps this could be the test for social media content.

You need only go on social media and see Democrats' campaign ads ranting at Republican extremism, only to conclude by asking for money. Money is not going to change the direction in which we are heading.

Using the media as the great bully pulpit doesn't cost anything. If Marjorie Taylor Greene, Matt Gaetz, Madison Cawthorn, etc., can get press play for every outlandish statement they make, why can't the Democrats, and others who see the dangers of authoritarianism before their very eyes, use the media to call out dangerous, hateful rhetoric? When elected leaders say they would rather support a white nationalist than a Democrat, where is the outrage? Why aren't these so-called leaders called on the carpet?

Judging by how much media attention is generated by Kevin McCarthy and Mitch McConnell, some might well think the Republican Party is in charge of Congress. House Speaker Nancy Pelosi and Senate Majority Leader Chuck Schumer seem to be AWOL; those in their charge seem paralyzed to act.

Misinformation, wild conspiratorial commentary…in fact, anything that defies logic, common sense, rational thought, etc., flourishes in a vacuum. When craziness in the form of anger and hatred is met with silence, craziness prevails.

Today's silent majority must not remain silent—indeed, it can't afford to. The Democrats, independents and common-sense moderate Republicans must join forces and mobilize the tens of millions who oppose authoritarianism through a common, coherent message that calls out dangerous rhetoric and blatant nonsense and re-instills what it means to be an American.

And this needs to be done now; time is of the essence.

ANOTHER DAY IN AMERICA

Our two major political parties are at each other's throats, so nothing gets done to address our nation's ills.

Social media, and a few national media outlets, have become a breeding ground for white supremacists and white nationalists to spread their bile, anger, and hatred.

Some influential public officials are giving aid and comfort to white supremacists and white nationalists. The number of officials appears to be growing.

Racial attacks are on the rise.

Ethnic attacks are on the rise.

Anti-Semitic attacks are on the rise.

Hate, anger, and rage have replaced civil discourse, with horrific consequences.

With open carry and "constitutional" carry, it is getting easier and easier to gain access not only to single-shot weapons, but automatic assault rifles capable of killing many.

People who in the past wouldn't have given a thought to going to a mall, shopping center or movie must now give pause.

Schools used to be a sanctuary, a place away from the daily trials and tribulations of the world; a place to learn and grow. Now, there are drills in the event of a shooting incident.

Remember when air travel was easy? Now, airports are security fortresses.

After each mass killing, we hear the same responses: "Horrible senseless act of violence." "Our thoughts and prayers are with the victims and their loved ones." Condolences in one form or another. There is outrage, but it passes.

Some clamor for something to be done, but nothing happens. Eventually, the shock wears off. There is no action; there is no change. And with each horror, we become more and more desensitized.

The status quo in the face of these mass killings only guarantees there will be more.

We try to convince ourselves that this doesn't represent who we really are; that the vitriolic rhetoric, and the racial, ethnic, and religious attacks and mass murders are isolated events. But grim statistics don't hide the fact that we are kidding ourselves if we believe this.

Some public officials are assaulting academic freedom and re-writing history to remove its harsh teachings. That number appears to be growing as well.

Intelligence, rational thinking, logic, common sense, wisdom are frowned upon. Epithets have replaced dialogue.

Fear is a form of imprisonment. If we don't leave our homes for fear of a crazed individual with a rifle, we are imprisoned.

We have a constitutionally recognized right of travel, but we can't exercise that right if we fear to leave our homes.

With this as our domestic situation, war drums are beating in Europe, and there remain daily threats from the Far East.

I don't have answers, but we elect our representatives to come up with them. And all the evidence points to an abysmal failure on their part.

I am certain of this much: our democratic republic is not sustainable under these circumstances. Just as individuals eventually crack under excess stress, so we as a nation are approaching stress overload. There is a tipping point.

We can hope, as Abraham Lincoln did, that our better angels will come forth, guide us, and save us and our nation. We can pray for divine guidance; perhaps for some miracle that will deliver us from our current plight. We can look to past crises—depression, war—that we survived and seek comfort in believing we will see our way through this.

Our vision would be clear if only those dark clouds would move out of the way.

SUPREME COURT HYPOCRISY

For decades, conservatives have argued that courts should interpret the Constitution and other law in keeping with its original meaning. Former President Trump's appointments to the Supreme Court — Neil Gorsuch, Brett Kavanaugh and Amy Coney Barrett — have described themselves as originalists, leading many to hope or fear that they would form a conservative majority with Chief Justice John Roberts, Justice Clarence Thomas, and Justice Samuel Alito. This has happened, although Roberts does not appear as ideologically committed as the other five. The recent leak of the abortion decision is clear evidence of this set conservative majority.

Originalism is a theory of the interpretation of legal texts, including the text of the Constitution. Originalists believe that the constitutional text ought to be given the original public meaning that it would have had at the time that it became law. Conservatives also refer to their interpretive approach as a form of textualism. This is a mode of interpretation that focuses on the plain meaning of the text of a legal document. Textualism usually emphasizes how the terms in the Constitution would be understood by people at the time they were ratified, as well as the context in which those terms appear. You can readily see the close relationship between these two interpretive methods.

Whenever Democrats refer to justices and judges who believe the law, in particular the Constitution, should be considered a living document that is to be interpreted in light of current times and circumstances, the Republicans declare this as "legislating from the bench." This they claim is heresy; they therefore seek Supreme Court justices who "will interpret the Constitution as written, and not as they would like it to read."

But the hypocrisy behind this claim is something conservative jurists deflect when confronted with their own examples of "legislating from the bench." Although there are several—including the famous or infamous Bush v. Gore of 2000—this commentary will address a significant one, a major one, and the latest one.

These three cases involve money as a form of free speech. As you read the rest of this narrative, ask yourself whether, when the framers of the First Amendment put the free speech language to paper, or when this amendment was adopted, they had in mind money as a form of speech.

In 1976, the Supreme Court in Buckley v. Valeo (1976) struck down limits on spending by campaigns and citizens but upheld the provision limiting the size of individual contributions to campaigns. Specifically, the Court said contribution ceilings did not violate the First Amendment but restrictions on campaign spending did. What is important here is the treatment of money in the form of campaign spending as a form of speech.

But it was not until 34 years later that the Court expressly discussed the relationship between campaign finance and free speech.

In the famous—or infamous—Citizens United v. Federal Elections Commission, 558 U.S. 310 (2010), the Court ruled that the free speech clause of the First Amendment prohibits the government from restricting independent expenditures for political campaigns by corporations, including nonprofit corporations, labor unions, and other associations.

A decision reached by the Court just the other day, Federal Elections Commission v. Cruz, was predictable in light of Citizens United. In a 6-3 decision, with all six conservatives voting as a bloc, the Court handed Texas Republican Sen. Ted Cruz a gift of $10,000.

Senator Cruz loaned his 2018 reelection campaign committee $260,000. After he won reelection, the campaign repaid him $250,000, and Senator Cruz and the committee sued in federal court, claiming that the limits on repaying the additional $10,000 were unconstitutional. A three-judge district court agreed "that the loan-repayment limitation burdens political speech without sufficient justification," and the FEC appealed directly to the Supreme Court.

The Supreme Court affirmed. The Court first held that Cruz and the committee have standing because "the Committee's present inability to repay the final $10,000 of Cruz's loans constitutes an injury in fact both to Cruz and to his Committee." On the merits, the Court first ruled that the repayment restriction “burdens core political speech without proper justification.”

Now for the hypocrisy. Nowhere in any of these three decisions is there any finding by these six originalists, supported by evidence, that the framers intended to treat money as free speech! Just a little legislating from the bench, eh?

In a classic case of the end justifying the means, if originalists need to depart from their interpretive roots to reach a pre-ordained conclusion, they will do so. Echoing Ralph Waldo Emerson: “A foolish consistency is the hobgoblin of little minds.”

REPUBLICANS, THIS IS ON YOU

Republicans seem to get a high when they point out Joe Biden’s gaffes, mistakes, and frustrations. They get a kick out of slogans that they believe point out his weaknesses and failings. Ok, that’s fair game. Democrats had four years of doing the same with Donald Trump. And since Trump knows nothing about silence, he’s still fair game for the Democrats. Of course, a few Republicans have joined them—those with some backbone and courage–and I don’t see any Democrats eager to join the Trump clown train, but that’s another matter.

What’s lost in this game of finger pointing is what the two major political parties actually stand for. I don’t mean their smooth-sounding rhetoric here; I mean by their actual conduct. Words without action is akin to vision without execution. The result is hallucination, according to Thomas Edison. The real question is what actions have the parties taken; this is the sine qua non of what they truly believe.

The Democrats essentially believe in a strong central government that preserves individual rights and freedom. The most glaring example is the New Deal legislation that was designed to deal with the Great Depression. Its latest example is Biden's Build Back Better plan, which includes massive infrastructure expenditures that are designed to repair long-neglected bridges, roadways, rail, etc.

The Republicans pass themselves off as the party of limited government and less taxes.

But here is where the rubber meets the road. There are Republican leaders in our federal and state governments who unabashedly tout support for white nationalism and white supremacy. They have taken out ads supporting the disgraced and factually flawed replacement theory. After a crazed white supremacist killed 10 blacks in a Buffalo supermarket, several Republicans walked back their support, saying they didn't understand what the replacement theory means. To accomplish this turnabout, they have to admit either being ignorant, indifferent, or just plain stupid--and hope their supporters don't know or don't care.

Today, Rep. Madison Cawthorn cares. He lost his bid for re-election because enough of the voters in his district believed he was too radical and reckless to serve in Congress. Imagine that; with the likes of Marjorie Taylor Greene and her ilk, Cawthorn was too much of an embarrassment.

So, to those Republicans who get a kick out of kicking Biden, let me ask you this: what elements of Republicanism that is clear and obvious today do you support?

Do you support less government? In Florida and in several states, the state governments are taking power away from local governments, including school boards. They are authorizing citizen lawsuits against local government. If the Democrats tried this, the Republicans would throw collective fits. Just look at Florida Gov. Ron DeSantis saying the state will take over the Disney financial mess he created. How about state governments imposing restrictions on academic freedom and speech on campuses? Other examples from other states abound. Are these examples of your support for less government?

Do you support less taxes? Influential Florida Sen. Rick Scott is on record as wanting to tax those currently not taxed, and raise taxes on the middle class, presumably to offset greater tax breaks for his, and his party's, wealthy corporate contributors. Is this your example of support for less taxes?

But let me be more direct here. Do you support white nationalism or white supremacy? Do you believe that whites are being replaced by minorities/immigrants?

Do you support racist, anti-Semitic rants and assaults? Republicans seem to be silent or tepid in their responses to the Buffalo, NY, mass shooting, and other threats against minorities. Do you support their silence?

Do you endorse the rhetoric of Senators Cruz, Hawley, Paul, Kennedy, Cotton, Graham, etc., and Reps. Jordan, McCarthy, Taylor Greene, Boebert, Gaetz, Gosar, etc. and Governors Abbott, DeSantis and Ducey, etc., who have voiced support for white nationalism, white supremacy, and replacement theory?

Or do you support Rep. Liz Cheney and others who have said, in Cheney's words: "The House GOP leadership has enabled white nationalism, white supremacy, and anti-Semitism. History has taught us that what begins with words ends in far worse. GOP leaders must renounce and reject these views and those who hold them." Do you believe Republicans must "renounce and reject these views and those who hold them?"

Do you still support Donald Trump, who infamously said there are some nice Neo-Nazis and white supremacists back in 2017? Remember Charlottesville?

Silence is complicity. It's also a sign of weakness—unless you agree. Republicans must show the backbone they claim Democrats don't have.

From the 1940s through the 1960s, the House Un-American Activities Committee (HUAC) took a prominent role in the investigation of communist activity in the United States. History tells us of the number of lives that were harmed, and careers ruined, as the committee members infamously intoned: "Are you now, or have you ever been, a member of the Communist Party?" The equally famous response usually was "I refuse to answer on the grounds that it might incriminate me," or "I plead the Fifth Amendment." Turning over every stone and looking behind every curtain to feed this witch hunt was an ugly, embarrassing time for the principles of American Democracy.

We can only wonder if this committee were in operation today whether its members would ask certain current members of Congress, state government leaders, etc., under oath, "Are you now, or have you ever been, a member of the Fascist Party, or a supporter of the fascist form of government?" How many do you think would answer "I refuse to answer on the grounds that it might incriminate me," or "I plead the Fifth Amendment?" Or considering the intelligence level, they might well answer "I don't know what fascism is."

REPUBLICANS: WHICH DOOR ARE YOU BEHIND?

Considering the state of the Republican Party over the last several years, and its status today, it is fair to ask to which faction of the Republican Party do adherents belong.

There seems to be three party factions out there. With apologies to that great television game show Let's Make a Deal, I'll refer to these factions behind doors. From the smallest to the largest, they are as follows:

Behind Door Number 1 is the group made up of Reps. Liz Cheney and Adam Kitzinger, and on occasion by Sen. Mitt Romney, and their followers who are mostly silent or extremely quiet in their support.

Behind Door Number 2 is the slightly larger group made up on rare occasions of Sen. Mitch McConnell and Rep. Kevin McCarthy (not to be confused with Charlie McCarthy, the woodenhead dummy of the 1930s to 1960s for ventriloquist Edgar Bergen, although there is certainly some similarity), except when they feel compelled to kiss the, ah, ring of their leader Donald Trump. McCarthy is more apt to act like this than McConnell, but the latter certainly has had his moments. Oh, I almost forgot...and the few who, in their saner moments, follow these two during their rare flashes of sanity, although these followers are also mostly silent or extremely quiet in their support.

Behind Door Number 3 is by far the largest group headed by Trump and his most vocal followers in Congress, consisting of Sens. Ted Cruz, Josh Hawley, Rand Paul, John Kennedy (not the former president; the Gomer Pyle act-alike from Louisiana), Tom Cotton, Lindsey Graham, etc., and Reps. Jim Jordan, Marjorie Taylor Greene, Lauren Boebert, Matt Gaetz, Mo Brooks, Paul Gosar, etc. and Governors Greg

Abbott (not to be confused with Bud Abbott of Abbott and Costello fame, although just as comedic), Ron DeSantis and Doug Ducey, etc. This group seems to have difficulty in trying to outshine such great historical luminaries as Elmer Fudd, Barney Fife, Forrest Gump, and Gomer Pyle in their frequent displays of simplemindedness. But that doesn't stop them from trying really hard to be serious—which only makes them look more clownish.

One of the two leaders of the first group has already announced his departure from Congress at the end of his current term. No doubt the third group, aided by many in the second, will try to elect additional flamethrowers, bigots, and conspiracy theorists to replace him—and others–who dared to challenge Trump and his acolytes; those who had the unmitigated gall, the effrontery, the audacity to show character, backbone, and strength; those who refused to show the weakness it takes to suck up to He Who Must Be Obeyed. Just what our nation needs, more elected officials like those behind Door Number 3!!

The leaders behind Door Number2 and 3 and will no doubt continue their weird ways for two reasons: first, they must not offend their leader You-Know-Who. But the second reason is more relevant and more draconian: some of those named above fancy themselves as the heir apparent once Trump leaves the scene. And they have proven their ability to get elected even while uttering the most outlandish, foolish, and dangerous things. Well, I don't know about Matt Gaetz yet. He might go the way of Madison Cawthorn, who fell into the Dunning-Kruger category: too stupid to know how stupid he is. Come to think of it, there are quite a few in the two larger factions who manifest the Dunning-Kruger effect. They are simply too stupid to know how stupid they are. Hopefully, the voters will feel embarrassed enough by their shenanigans to send them the way of Madison Cawthorn.

So, while those behind all three doors engage in their internal culture war for control of the Republican Party, and as we move toward the November election cycle, it's fair to ask those who identify themselves as Republicans what they mean by that. In other words, which group behind which door do they support? And if they answer either Door Number 2 or Number 3, why?

IS THIS WHAT CONSERVATIVES REALLY WANT FOR AMERICA?

Conservatives, now largely made up of right-wing extremists, enjoy bashing President Biden as a feeble demented socialist who hasn't accomplished anything. Well, I certainly admit it's impossible to get the Republicans to pass any legislation that will "make Biden look good," and compared to the far-right extremists, even moderates might appear to them to be socialists. Those who make this claim show they don't really know what socialism is, but that's another story.

The feeble demented claim is laughable considering the intellectual powerhouses of Donald Trump and his merry band of madmen and madwomen. Repeated lies, fact deniers, crazy conspiracy theories, leading attacks on the capital, etc., are not marks of brilliance. But that, too, is another story.

As the right vents their bile at all things they dislike, the question that must be asked is a simple one: what do conservatives really want?

With a legally elected Democrat president, conservatives can't be too thrilled with our democratic republic. But what is their plan to replace the status quo? What do they want that will bring fellow likeminded rightists into our federal and state governments?

There is no longer any effort to disguise the right wing's goal: an authoritarian fascist-style state.

Oh, there will be free elections of course.... just like the free elections in Russia, North Korea, China....and Hungary. It can't happen here, you say? Well, it is happening. Just look at the election laws that have been rewritten in many red states. And if that doesn't do the trick, then just re-write the Constitution through a constitutional convention. That's provided for in the Constitution itself. Under Article V, Congress is required to convene a constitutional convention if two-thirds of state legislatures (34 states) call for one. This is not an insurmountable burden for an authoritarian government.

Hungary is special. Historian and author Heather Cox Richardson hits the nail on the head when she describes precisely what American conservatives want. Here is her analysis in full. As you read her report below, ask yourself if this is what you want for America.

Conservatives will no doubt deny this as just some liberal rabblerousing, but in the immortal words of Jack Nicholson, they simply "can't handle the truth." Here is her report in full:

"The Conservative Political Action Committee (CPAC), the influential right-wing PAC of the American Conservative Union, is holding its first European event, convening today in Budapest, Hungary. Its leaders have chosen Hungary apparently because they see that country as a model for the society they would like to see in the U.S. under a strongman leader like rising authoritarian prime minister Viktor Orbán of Hungary.

Orbán is the architect of what he calls "illiberal democracy," or "Christian democracy." This form of government holds nominal elections, although their outcome is preordained because the government controls all the media and has silenced opposition. Illiberal democracy rejects modern liberal democracy because the equality it champions means an acceptance of immigrants, LGBTQ rights, and women's rights and an end to traditionally patriarchal society. Orbán's model of minority rule promises a return to a white-dominated, religiously based society, and he has pushed his vision by eliminating the independent press, cracking down on political opposition, getting rid of the rule of law, and dominating the economy with a group of crony oligarchs.

Led by personalities like Tucker Carlson, the American right wing embraces the Hungarian model, despite the corruption, lack of legal accountability, and attacks on the press that make Hungary the only member of the European Union no longer rated as "free" by democracy watchdog Freedom House. As if in illustration of Orbán's policies, U.S. journalists were not allowed into CPAC today.

Orbán gave the keynote speech at the CPAC convention. In it, he embraced the "great replacement theory" that says white people are being replaced by immigrants of color. This is the myth that motivated the shooter in Buffalo, New York, last weekend, when he murdered ten people and wounded three others. It is the myth from which most Republicans have tried to distance themselves since the Buffalo killings.

And yet, when CPAC leader Matt Schlapp met U.S. journalists outside, he said that ending abortion rights would address the great replacement myth: "If you say there is a population problem in a country, but you're killing millions of your own people through legalized abortion every year, if that were to be reduced, some of that problem is solved," Schlapp said. "You have millions of people who can take many of these jobs. How come no one brings that up? If you're worried about this quote-unquote replacement, why don't we start there? Start with allowing our own people to live."

Orbán told the attendees that the right wing in Europe and the United States must fight together to "reconquer" institutions in Brussels and Washington, D.C., before the 2024 election because those "liberals" who currently control them are destroying western civilization.

It is surprising to see folks who talk about American greatness take their inspiration from the leader of a small central European country of fewer than 10 million people, about the size of Michigan. Yale philosophy professor Jason Stanley commented: "Oh come on US conservatives, stop embarrassing yourselves. Have some dignity and national pride."

Is this what you want America to be?

THIS IS HOW IT STARTS

A Virginia Beach attorney and state delegate and his client, a right-wing republican running for Congress, are suing Barnes & Noble for engaging in the business of selling books.

A Facebook post by the attorney says his client has directed him "to seek a restraining order against Barnes and Noble and Virginia Beach Schools to enjoin them from selling or loaning books (a state judge found probable cause to believe are obscene) to minors without parent consent."

What should send chills up and down the spines of all Americans who value our democratic republic is the following statement.

No longer is this about the rights of students to access books. **It's now about the rights of private businesses to sell books.** This attorney suggests this is a new avenue for parents to fight.

"We are in a major fight. Suits like this can be filed all over Virginia. There are dozens of books. Hundreds of schools," he said.

Read that quote from the attorney again. Dozens of books; hundreds of schools, in Virginia today. Tomorrow, there will be many more books, in many more schools, in many more states. And many more booksellers.

That's it. The self-appointed censors with their self-serving moral code will tell us who can sell books and which ones we can read. It starts with a few carefully selected books. But where does it end? If this attorney and his likeminded ilk have their way, the government will tell us what we can read, and what businesses can sell which books.

This following is from the United States Holocaust Memorial Museum:

"On May 10, 1933, student groups at universities across Germany carried out a series of book burnings of works that the students and leading Nazi party members associated with an "un-German spirit." Enthusiastic crowds witnessed the burning of books by Brecht, Einstein, Freud, Mann and Remarque, among many other well-known intellectuals, scientists and cultural figures, many of whom were Jewish. The largest of these book bonfires occurred in Berlin, where an estimated 40,000 people gathered to hear a speech by the propaganda minister, Joseph Goebbels, in which he pronounced that "Jewish intellectualism is dead" and endorsed the students' "right to clean up the debris of the past."

The response to the book burnings was immediate and widespread. Counter demonstrations took place in New York and other American cities, including Philadelphia, Cleveland, and Chicago. Journalists in the American and world press expressed shock and dismay at these attacks on German intellectual freedom, and various authors wrote in support of their assaulted German brethren. Artists, writers, doctors, and other intellectuals fled Germany, prompted by the barbarity of the book burnings and by continuing acts of Nazi persecution.

Such barbarity was just the beginning, however. One can see in retrospect how the book burnings and other steps to remove "Jewish influence" from German institutions foreshadowed much more catastrophic Nazi plans for the Jews of Europe. Eerily, among the books consigned to the flames in 1933 were the works of the nineteenth century Jewish poet Heinrich Heine, who in 1822 penned the prophetic words, 'Where they burn books, they will, in the end, burn human beings too.'"

The Virginia lawyer is, of course, claiming his action is in support of freedom, in this case, parental freedom. His definition of freedom, however, is warped. Stripped of its gloss, he means freedom to censor, freedom to control the publishing business. Freedom to have others tell us what we can and cannot read. Freedom to impose his moral code on the rest of us. All that is needed are right wing jurists to buy into this blatant censorship that trashes the First Amendment's freedom of speech and press.

Our democracy depends on an informed citizenry. If books are banned, and then destroyed, sources of knowledge are destroyed. And if history, science, and literature are destroyed, so is the ability to learn the harsh lessons of history so we don't repeat them. And we lose our ability to advance through science and enhance our culture through the creative arts.

If a parent doesn't want to have his/her child read a book, all that is necessary is for the parent to exercise responsible parenting over the child. The parent cannot and must not be permitted to control what others decide to read, or what a publisher desires to sell.

After this round of book banning, there will no doubt be others. Books that make people feel psychological discomfort about their history is fair game. In fact, anything they don't like is fair game. And after the censors realize that banned books are still available, especially on cellphones and tablets, history tells us what follows.

Where does it end?

Can you hear the faint sounds of goose steps in the background? You will as they grow louder.

THE MYTH OF ASSAULT RIFLE SELF-DEFENSE

We know that the United States is the only country in the world where the number of firearms exceeds the total population; current data puts the number of firearms at roughly 120 for every 100 people. We also know that gun ownership is expanding and will continue to do so as fear causes more and more into believing a weapon is necessary for self-defense.

There are statistics that show the actual use of a firearm for self-defense hovers around one percent, but the NRA hastens to point out that what is missing here is the intimidation factor; that is, a person intending to commit a crime will forgo it if he fears the potential victim is armed. That is certainly a fair assumption.

The debate about firearms, however, is not about possession and ownership; the Second Amendment and the Heller decision by the Supreme Court make these clear. Rather, the debate is—and should be–about access to, and ownership and possession of, a particular type of weapon that has been used repeatedly in mass murders committed by a lone gunman.

That weapon is the AR-15 and its kind.

Since self-defense is the most prevalent reason given for gun ownership, it's fair to ask how many times an AR-15 or similar style firearm has been used by the owner in self-defense. I tried to Google this and couldn't get a number. I believe I know why. If the purpose of carrying such a weapon is to intimidate, I haven't seen any statistics on this precise intimidation factor. I daresay there isn't a person out there who has ever seen anyone carrying this type of weapon to intimidate or knows of anyone who has used it in self-defense.

That's because this type of weapon is not a firearm designed for self-defense. It can't be concealed like a pistol. It is an assault weapon, designed to eliminate as many people as possible. It works for the military and in some law enforcement situations; it is not designed as a weapon for private personal use.

The Heller decision provides no comfort for those who believe the Second Amendment protects the assault weapon owner. As Justice Scalia said: "Although we do not undertake an exhaustive historical analysis today of the full scope of the Second Amendment, nothing in our opinion should be taken to cast doubt on longstanding prohibitions on the possession of firearms by felons and the mentally ill, or laws forbidding the carrying of firearms in sensitive places such as schools and government buildings, or laws imposing conditions and qualifications on the commercial sale of arms." Interestingly, so far, courts have excluded concealed carry from constitutional protection, relying on Scalia's observation that "the majority of the 19th-century courts to consider the question held that prohibitions on carrying concealed weapons were lawful under the Second Amendment or state analogues."

Scalia was the Court's supreme originalist, looking to the original intent of the Second Amendment when adopted in determining its meaning today. It is self-evident that at that time, there were no automatic assault weapons such as the AR-15. Those making a claim that the framers of the Constitution intended to include the assault rifle, or that this weapon of mass killing is accorded the same constitutional protection as the pistol are fooling no one, except perhaps themselves.

The legislative branch remains free to regulate these assault weapons. What is lacking is the courage to act. The gun lobby and their loyalists in government will rage until they are red in the face over someone threatening a Supreme Court justice, but for the families that lost loved ones to the madness of an AR-15 carrier, it's just thoughts and prayers.

The obvious question is who needs an AR-15 for self-defense? The answer is no one.

Assault weapons do not belong on the street or in people's homes. We have had enough horrific examples to make this self-evident. If our government fails to act, we can expect these types of attacks to continue. How many more school children must we lose? How many more shoppers or moviegoers will it take to finally get some action to deal with this particular type of weapon?

There are those who believe that once one type of weapon is banned, others bans will follow. The Second Amendment and its jurisprudence, however, make it clear that this belief is based on fear, not law or fact.

WHAT WILL BECOME OF IT?

The House Committee investigating the January 6, 2021, attack on our nation's capital is poised to hold public hearings on its findings. The committee, with only two courageous Republican Party members—the party as a whole long ago decided not to give any credence to the investigation and its findings—has interviewed almost 1000 people—including those subpoenaed—and gathered 100,000 pages of documents.

The findings are expected to be comprehensive and damning. Words such as "insurrection," "sedition," and "treason" will no doubt appear in one descriptive form or another.

We already know much of what took place leading up to, and immediately following, January 6. What we will now see is a precise timeline with names of players and their activities.

All of this is a big problem for the Republican Party. Already, the extreme right that now controls the party has lined up its most bombastic members to rant, rave and do their best to otherwise deflect from the findings and, hopefully, conclusions.

The Department of Justice and the several United States Attorney's Offices will be on high alert to take heed of these findings and act according to the law. That's their job. Our democracy requires that they do their job.

This leads to what is most critical question that must be asked once the committee's work is done: what will become of it?

Will the report be met with Republican ho-hum, just another witch hunt or hatchet job the public will buy? Will enough people really care enough to make certain such a dark blot on our nation's history never happens again?

Or will there be a day of reckoning for lawbreakers, those who claim to be anti-crime and pro law and order so long as they aren't the ones charged with criminal behavior?

We will most likely find out that certain elected and appointed public officials were complicit in engaging in criminal conduct, perhaps conspiratorial criminal conduct. Will these findings be whitewashed, shoved under the rug, and treated as, in the words of the Republican National Committee, just some officials supporting zealous Trump supporters engaging in legitimate political discourse?

What happened before, during and after January 6 was built entirely on a lie of a rigged election that the right bought lock, stock, and barrel (no pun intended.) These zealots, who claim the high road on logic and knowledge, have repeatedly displayed neither in their blind, diehard support for the repeated falsehood that has now reached the historic level of being dubbed the Big Lie. Imagine that; being famous for uttering the biggest lie of all! Yet, even after every court in the nation rejected every claim, millions still hold fast to it. And they have the audacity to call their opponents ignorant and misguided!

The answer to the question I pose depends on how loud, vocal, and persistent we are as a nation in saving our democratic republic. Will almost 250 years of our grand experiment in self-governance reach its end, in favor of an authoritarian form of government where it decides what we say, think and do? Will those public officials implicated in criminal conduct and are on the ballot in November be returned to office despite their aberrant conduct? Or will we collectively say, "lesson learned" and prosecute the lawbreakers as well as pass laws to prevent a repeat of January 6, or worse?

We will find out soon enough.

THIS DISEASE IS DESTROYING US

Bill Maher had a wonderful and poignant opening segment the other day, questioning whether our nation can continue as a democratic republic when there is a disease running rampant that affects tens of millions. That disease is stupidity.

The comedian, actor, political commentator, and television host used Jay Leno's "man on the street" type of interviews to make his point, talking to randomly chosen people and asking them basic questions that anyone should be able to answer. The answers shown were embarrassments, to say the least. What is the largest country? Asia. Where is Queen Elizabeth from? Egypt. You get the idea. The answers caused Maher to ask what students are actually being taught, and whether we're too stupid to continue as a nation.

What is a far more serious concern, however, is the steadfast belief system evident in the face of the latest revelations about the January 6, 2021, attack on our nation's capital by insurrectionists hellbent on overthrowing our government and installing Donald Trump as president.

The first hearing by the House committee investigating this assault, televised the other night, was riveting, to say the least. Using testimony from Trump supporters, the evidence was clear that the attack was planned, orchestrated, and carried out at the direction of President Trump, who knew he was feeding his supporters a lie about a rigged election. Trump was told repeatedly by his own staffers that there was no evidence of fraud sufficient to change the election results. Trump knew he lost, yet he fed a gullible crowd of right-wing extremists his Big Lie, and they bought it hook, line and sinker, resulting in death and destruction. Trump even supported those who threatened to hang his vice president, Mike Pence.

Trump continued his assault on truth and the mayhem he launched even after losing every single lawsuit he and his supporters filed—more than 60 of them. Without a single fact to support his Big Lie, he nevertheless persists in uttering it to this day, even to the point of throwing his daughter Ivanka under the bus for daring to question him.

Yet, despite the clear, unequivocal evidence presented by the committee, public reaction thus far has been tepid. In fact, some people in Pennsylvania referred to the hearing as "rubbish," adding that "all they're trying to do is isolate Trump and pick on all of his friends. They want to find him guilty of something."

How many others feel this same way? How many others are content to simply dismiss all of this damning evidence as "rubbish" or some other word that requires no thought, no analysis, no acceptance of fact?

Historically, we have prided ourselves as being an educated, informed people. We rely on facts, logic, common sense in exercising rational judgment. Or at least we used to.

What has happened to us that we allow dismissive words such as "rubbish" to replace fact? What happened to us that allows raw opinion based solely on belief—however flawed—to replace logic, common sense, and rational thinking?

To be sure, there will always be people who believe what they want, regardless of those pesky things called facts. They will readily accept an alternate universe akin to Newspeak of George Orwell's dystopian novel 1984. But the sheer number of these people into the tens of millions who confidently feel this way should send shock waves across the country.

When science is questioned. When intelligence becomes a dirty word. When ignorance is treated as knowledge, our nation suffers. Dumbing down has become fashionable. For them, it has simply become too much of a task, too much of an effort, to actually think things through.

Instead of bolstering our education system, there are forces at work to prevent teaching of certain subjects that are designed to make us a better people. When knowledge is perverted, when subjects that cause psychological distress are banned, something is dreadfully wrong with our education system, and those who are charged with assuring an informed and intelligent populace going forward.

The evidence is clear that something is dreadfully wrong with our education system that allows for, and even rewards, ignorance, indifference, and stupidity.

Considering the sheer number of people who will dismiss any and all facts to the contrary and continue their steadfast support of the Big Lie (as well as others), stupidity should be treated as a public health emergency.

HYPOCRISY IN THE TREATMENT OF FUNDAMENTAL RIGHTS

It is worth noting the rank hypocrisy behind how two fundamental rights are treated differently by Republicans in Congress, state legislatures and the courts.

Fundamental rights are a group of rights that have been recognized as being accorded the highest degree of protection from encroachment by the courts. These rights are specifically identified in the constitution, or have been found under due process of law.

The two foundational rights involved here are the right to vote and the right to bear arms.

As the Supreme Court said in Reynolds v. Sims: "The right to vote freely for the candidate of one's choice is of the essence of a democratic society, and any restrictions on that right strike at the heart of representative government. [...] Undoubtedly, the right of suffrage is a fundamental matter in a free and democratic society. That the right to vote is so fundamental as to require no elaboration is further demonstrated by the language of three amendments: The Fifteenth, Nineteenth and Twenty-sixth Amendments say so in unmistakably clear language. The Fifteenth (dealing with race, color, or previous condition of servitude) and Nineteenth (sex discrimination) both begin with these same 10 words: "The right of citizens of the United States to vote…". The Nineteenth (18 years of age) says "The right of citizens of the United States….to vote…." Without any doubt, the right to vote is fundamental in our society.

Similarly, as recognized by the Supreme Court in District of Columbia v. Heller and interpreted in the lower courts, the Second Amendment exhibits all the hallmarks of a fundamental constitutional right. It is a non-economic, individual dignity right that is considered "implicit in the concept of ordered liberty."

Thus, we have two rights each declared fundamental by our nation's highest court.

Remember that a fundamental right is subject to the least amount of restriction or limitation, and any limitation must be viewed by the court under a strict scrutiny standard. Strict scrutiny is the highest form of judicial review that courts use to evaluate the constitutionality of laws, regulations, or other governmental policies under legal challenge. As Justice David Souter famously wrote in his dissenting opinion in Alameda Books v. City of Los Angeles, "Strict scrutiny leaves few survivors." This means that when a court evaluates the constitutionality of a law using the strict scrutiny standard, the court will usually strike down the law.

In short, The government, in justifying a law seeking to implicate a fundamental right, must show that the law is supported by a compelling government interest, and the law must be narrowly tailored or is the least restrictive means to meet that interest.

Now for the hypocrisy. Relying on the argument that the fundamental right to keep and bear arms doesn't allow for many restrictions, efforts are under way by conservatives to expand Second Amendment rights to, among other things, allow for open carry of firearms in public places and extending this amendment's coverage to assault weapons—far beyond the types used at the time of the adoption of this amendment. This same defense is being used to strike at the heart of any commonsense legislation placing limits on the availability of weapons to the general public.

Simultaneously, rejecting the same type of fundamental right argument by the left when applied to the right to vote, these same forces are seeking to restrict or suppress the exercise of this right through targeted measured aimed at distinct and historically recognized voting patterns.

So far, the courts either have not treated these fundamental rights under the same interpretive standard or have ignored the notion that what's good for the goose must be good for the gander.

The bottom line is that the judiciary cannot legitimately consider two fundamental rights by using different interpretive standards. Simply put, the courts can't allow for expansion of one fundamental right while allowing for restriction or suppression of another without being called out on it. Justice requires fundamental fairness; this kind of disparate treatment strikes at the heart of the principle of equal justice under the law.

MIND YOUR OWN BUSINESS

A major problem that lies at the heart of our national divide is that there are too many who, being convinced that they have the inside track on righteousness, want to impose their beliefs on the rest of us in part by electing like-minded people who will do their dirty work.

To be sure, there must be a consensus on certain things that we expect our government to provide. The preamble to our Constitution sets out what they are: to "establish justice, insure domestic tranquility, provide for the common defense, promote the general welfare, and secure the blessings of liberty to ourselves and our posterity….". Explicit in this broad grant is the protection of the health, safety, and welfare of the people.

But when any group uses its belief system to assume the mantle of superiority and then uses that system as a platform to dictate how others should think, believe, and act, we have a dangerous situation that threatens the foundation of our government and way of life.

What makes this so onerous is that the belief system need not be based on fact, logic, rational thought, or common sense. In fact, in most cases, it's not. When a belief system drives opinion which in turn drives action, that action has no foundation in fact. Without such a foundation, people are free to believe whatever they wish, and then seek to impose that on everyone else. The danger of this scenario to our democratic institutions should be self-evident. The history of the last 100 years is clear evidence of the path we must avoid at all costs.

We see examples of this just about every day. Attacking knowledge by rewriting and sanitizing history, clamping down on academic freedom, and dissing science in favor of pure belief or junk science. Punishing dissent or disagreement. Restricting the fundamental right to vote. These are basic rights protected by our Constitution, yet we see examples of perversions of these rights right before our eyes.

The fact that a majority of Americans support certain governmental actions means nothing if a number of officials are bought and paid for by wealthy lobbyists, or religious groups whose influence is greater than their numbers. When we move away from the will of the people to the will of a religious organization or narrow special interest group, the result is an authoritarian, fascist-type government.

These groups may well profess a "live and let live" view, but that's bogus. If it were true, abortion would be solely a matter between a woman and her doctor. And issues about gun regulation wouldn't be met with the hackneyed notion that people need an assault rifle for self-protection, or the nonsense that once the government starts regulating, it will go after all weapons.

The reality is that the Second Amendment protects the right to keep and bear arms. That takes care of the nonsensical notion. And there is absolutely no evidence that carrying an assault rifle provides any measure of self-defense protection. Moreover, as the Heller decision makes abundantly clear, there is no constitutional right to keep and bear an AR-15 or its kind. But powerful lobbyists who contribute mightily to certain members of Congress and state legislators have convinced those who are bought lock, stock, and barrel (pun intended) not to enact any legislation that would ban these weapons of mass murder.

Fortunately, there is a sure way to counteract this belief over fact syndrome. When someone makes an alarming statement, check it out. Is it fact or opinion? If offered as opinion, what is the basis for it? If offered as fact, what is the foundation for it? Read. Analyze. Draw a conclusion that is supported by reason, logic, common sense, and sound judgment.

And above all, ask questions. When someone makes a statement that is opinion masquerading as fact, ask what the basis is. What facts support the opinion? What is the supporting rationale? Those who spew emotive words designed to anger can't handle being questioned. Question them vigorously. If they walk away in a huff, keep after them. They know they've been caught and can't handle the truth of their pandering or ignorance.

Avoid at all costs accepting an opinion devoid of fact as reality. We know people died because they accepted a lie as truth. Just go back to January 6 of last year. We are supposed to be an enlightened people. We need to act like we are, and stop allowing the nonsensical, uninformed, and unintelligent to carry the day. Those who behave this way need to be called out in no uncertain terms. Enough is enough!

Remind them of the old adage: Mind your own business!

THE "I'M A BS ARTIST AND YOU'RE AN IDIOT" DEFENSE

A clip from yesterday's televised House January 6 committee meeting brought to mind the incredible defense put forth by right-wing lawyer Sidney Powell, as well Fox pundit Tucker Carlson.

You might recall that voting machine company Dominion Voting Systems sued Powell for defamation after she vigorously pushed lawsuits and appeared before conservative media on behalf of Donald Trump claiming fraud; that the election was stolen because Dominion used technology that could switch votes away from Trump, technology linked to communist Venezuela to help steal elections for Hugo Chavez, and Georgia officials were active participants in the fraud.

In her defense, Powell, through her lawyers, made the argument that "no reasonable person would conclude that (her) statements were truly statements of fact," and that she was just offering her opinion on a matter of great public importance and that, therefore, her comments should be protected by the First Amendment. In other words, she's just a BS artist who can't be taken seriously. Imagine that; a lawyer who can't be taken seriously. She should be permanently disbarred as a blight to the legal profession.

This is the same defense offered by Fox News Host Tucker Carlson. The lawsuit in Carlson's case was brought by Karen McDougal, a former Playboy model who claimed Carlson defamed her by saying she extorted President Trump out of $150,000 in exchange for her silence about an alleged affair.

That's right. Carlson's lawyers argued that viewers can't believe what Carlson offers as facts. He's literally a BS artist masquerading as someone who knows what he's talking about. This defense worked for Carlson and Fox

News: the defamation lawsuit was dismissed by a Trump-appointed federal judge. Why this BS artist who is playing his audience remains on the air is a mystery. Wait, no it's not; it's all about ratings, and Carlson draws millions into his web of deceit.

Even Rudy Giuliani relied on this defense, as have others who spread lies about a rigged election that led to a failed coup attempt, lies that incredibly still resonate to this day. Despite what we're learning from these televised hearings, millions still cling to the lies and threaten further violence if any of the perpetrators are criminally charged for their dangerous charade. Giuliani can no longer practice law; his license is suspended and, considering his overall behavior, is most likely incompetent to practice anyway.

This, from the party that prides itself on individual accountability and responsibility. Powell, Carlson, and Giuliani are neither accountable nor responsible for their words because they are not to be believed. This defense makes a mockery of their claim to being the party of law and order.

This defense gives cover to the outlandish, the lunacy, the madness, and puts the blame squarely on the audience, rather than the speaker. This is a dangerous defense because it shifts the blame from the deliberate actors to the most gullible and naive among us.

In essence, if this defense is available to those who foment anger and hate, then the obvious question is who can you believe? And if you choose to believe them and act on their words, you face the consequences, not them.

The sad fact is that tens of millions believed what these clowns said back then and continue to believe their BS lies to this day. Five people died on the attack on the nation's capital on January 6 because an audience of gullible lemmings acted on inflammatory words the Powells, Carlsons and Giulianis of the far right uttered to their obedient masses.

Powell, Carlson, and Giuliani are very clear in what they think of their respective audiences: you are fools, idiots, and morons for believing what we say. Yes, what we said was to make you angry, mad, and vengeful. Yes, we did this deliberately. But we're not responsible if you choose to act on our words and destroy property and put people's lives in danger. After all, we are not to be believed.

Is this what conservatives mean when they talk about promoting conservative values. Their silence speaks loudly.

A sad commentary about far too many members of a political party that used to stand for some decent principles.

What is most glaringly incredible about Carlson's defense is what he is saying about his audience. Based on his own words, those who listen to him and believe what he says are unreasonable; that is, not guided by or based on good sense. Synonyms for "unreasonable" include absurd, arbitrary, biased, contradictory, foolish, illogical, inconsistent, irrational, preposterous, senseless, silly, stupid, wrong, excessive, exorbitant, extreme, illegitimate, improper, inordinate, unconscionable. Can you imagine anyone in the media calling his audience these things? Yet, this is Tucker Carlson's take on his followers. Of course, it's possible that those who watch his show don't believe what he says and are therefore, by his own definition, reasonable people. But that begs the question why anyone would watch his show if they didn't believe a word he says. Fox pays him millions to sling his BS because he has a large audience willing to swallow it.

NOVEMBER LOOMS OMINOUS

This November, we will for the first time be able to gauge the size of the electorate that supports Donald Trump and Trumpism in all of its manifestations.

For them, all of his factually documented peccadillos, failings and even crimes will not matter. It will not matter that he fomented an insurrection designed to prevent the orderly constitutional transfer of power from the election loser to the winner. It will not matter that his initial response to COVID was inept and tragic. It will not matter that he tried to secure help in his re-election bid by asking a foreign government for assistance. His pathological lying will not matter. His two impeachments will not matter. The findings and conclusions of the House January 6 investigation will not matter.

For them, facts that counter their belief system don't matter. Science doesn't matter. History doesn't matter.

For his loyalists, Trump is truth. Trump is righteousness. Trump is law and order. Trump is justice. Trump is patriotism. Trump is honesty.

What matters are alternate facts, junk science, re-writing history, re-writing or re-interpreting the law to secure favorable outcomes. And on and on. Everything that cuts into their rigid mindset is fake news, lies, witch hunts, hatchet jobs, etc.

If yesterday's election results represent a snapshot of what to expect in November, everything we have learned about Trump and Trumpism over the past five-plus years will not matter much to his ardent supporters. And it won't matter whether his support is genuine or simply out of fear. The outcome will be the same.

Recall Trump's own words: "I alone can fix it." "Stable genius." "Perfect phone call." "I'm the most successful person ever to run for the presidency, by far. Nobody's ever been more successful than me. I'm the most successful person ever to run." "Sorry losers and haters, but my IQ is one of the highest - and you all know it! Please don't feel so stupid or insecure, it's not your fault." "I could stand in the middle of 5th Avenue and shoot somebody, and I wouldn't lose voters." "Nobody has better respect for intelligence than Donald Trump." "What you're seeing and what you're reading is not what's happening." "The only way we're going to lose this election is if the election is rigged, remember that. It's the only way we're going to lose this election."

History teaches the consequences when the masses give their undying support to a single authoritarian figure, especially one who exhibits a narcissistic personality disorder, demonstrated by a pattern of self-centered, arrogant thinking and behavior, a lack of empathy and consideration for other people, and an excessive need for admiration. Others often describe people with this disorder as cocky, manipulative, selfish, patronizing, and demanding.

The relationship between the anointed leader and his diehards is called the cult of leadership, whereby the populace creates an idealized and heroic image of a leader, often through unquestioning flattery and praise. The cult is typically a group or movement held together by a shared commitment to a single charismatic leader and/or ideology. It has a belief system that has the answers to all of life's questions and offers a special solution to be gained only by following the leader's rules.

Does this ring a bell? It certainly should.

Soon, the November elections and the tealeaf reading that follows will be history. The overriding question that could well follow is what is to become of our democratic institutions if we replace what has sustained our nation for almost 250 years with a cult of leadership, along with a complicit Congress and judicial system, and with copycat systems at the state level?

Do we really want our nation to move in the cult of leadership direction? And what are we to do about it?

DEPLORABLE

When Donald Trump first announced his candidacy for president, a large number of potential voters believed that being a successful businessman, he would bring his business acumen to the White House and our nation would be the beneficiary of his knowledge and skills.

I wonder whether they feel the same way today. However, that really is of no import anymore. What is important is, after all we have learned about him over the past five-plus years, what still makes him a viable candidate in 2024? What is it about him that still deserves the blind adoration of so many?

If you were asked to describe in one word the behavior of Trump, his loyalists and MAGA supporters today, what word would you use?

How would you describe a president who:

*violated the law by asking a foreign government for help in his re-election bid?

*conspired with others to cause a riot that came dangerously close to a coup?

*lied about an election result, and continues to lie about it to this day, despite the absence of a single shred of evidence to support his lie?

*has repeatedly challenged and put at risk democratic principles and guardrails in part by branding the media the enemy of the people?

*has made sexist, racist, homophobic, etc., comments?

*has given aid and comfort to domestic terrorists, considered by our national security forces as the most dangerous threat to our country today?

*repeatedly dissed our long-standing allies in favor of endorsing dictators like Vladimir Putin and Kim Jong-il?

The list goes on and on.

What word would you use to describe the conduct those members of Congress, governors, state elections officials and legislators, and other public officers who take an oath to defend the constitution and affirm the view that a public office is a public trust, yet steadfastly continue to support Trump despite what they know about him? What do call those who say they support white nationalists over democrats?

Recently, authorities arrested 31 members of the white supremacist group Patriot Front near an Idaho pride event after they were found packed into the back of a U-Haul truck with riot gear. Instead of applauding the efforts of law enforcement in protecting the lives of innocent citizens, a number of anonymous callers threatened law enforcement for daring to arrest these white supremacists.

What are we to make of these domestic terrorists and those who threaten law enforcement for arresting them? Recall that these are folks who are supposed to represent law and order. Threatening law enforcement personnel for doing their job is not what law and order is all about. What word would you use to describe the conduct of both the group members and the anonymous callers?

Recall that in 2017 after the violence in Charlottesville, Virginia, Trump said there were some nice Neo-Nazis, and right after the January 6 riot at the capital, Trump told his supporters "we love you."

Again, what word would you use to describe this behavior?

That word is deplorable. It means deserving of censure or contempt. Hillary Clinton made a mistake in referred to a "basket of deplorables" during the 2016 presidential campaign. She was referring to Trump's supporters as a group, rather than to their demonstrated behavior.

The conduct described above is not normal and must never become normalized or accepted. It's not befitting the person holding the highest office in the land. It's not befitting of those who have taken an oath to defend the constitution. It's not befitting for those who swear or affirm that a public office is a public trust. It is categorically deplorable.

Planning a riot and threatening law enforcement for doing their job is not normal and must never become normalized. It, too, is categorically deplorable.

Donald Trump, to his everlasting shame, gave voice to the forces of darkness. He alone made it fashionable for right wing extremists to emerge from their caves and practice their hatred and anger in public places. It's time for our voices of sanity to send them back from whence they came.

For the Republican Party that prides itself as the party of law and order, stands for personal responsibility and accountability, and presses conservative values, it must hold accountable those whose behavior is deplorable. The party's legitimacy, as well as our democratic foundations, are at stake.

WHERE ARE THE SO-CALLED "PATRIOTS" NOW?

We learned from the latest hearing by the House Committee investigating the January 6 attack on the capital how close we came to an actual coup overturning the will of the people.

Recall that President Donald Trump on that fateful date implored his vice president, Mike Pence, to reject election results legally certified by the several states and either send them back to the states for re-certification, or simply declare his president re-elected. This, despite the fact that both the popular and Electoral College vote were in favor of Joe Biden.

In demanding that Pence "do the right thing" and thereby preserve our Constitution and democracy, we know now that Trump and his allies were perverting both. The country he asked his loyalists to preserve is not our country; it's the kind of country we associate with dictators and despots.

Trump called the rioters and his allies "patriots" for standing up to the rule of law. Now, 18 months later, let's see where those loyal "patriots" are.

Hundreds of those who stormed the capital are either in jail or facing prosecution and jail time.

Trump's lawyer and former New York City Mayor Rudy Giuliani has been suspended from the practice of law. He may well be permanently disbarred, and he faces potential criminal charges.

Trump lawyer John Eastman is the subject of a California Bar complaint, has plead the Fifth Amendment repeatedly during the House committee investigation, and faces an uncertain future both professionally and in the criminal justice system. He also asked for a pardon from Trump.

Trump lawyer Sidney Powell is the subject of a Texas Bar complaint and may well face additional consequences for her outlandish conduct following the November 2020 presidential election.

Several Trump loyalists, including Steve Bannon and Pete Navarro, have defied congressional subpoenas and have been indicted for contempt of Congress.

Several members of Congress whose names have floated as being complicit in Trump's efforts to forge ahead with his rigged election lies have refused to testify under oath before the House committee.

Their status under our criminal justice system remains up in the air at this time.

How many loyalists have asked Trump for a pardon remains an open question.

And Donald Trump, who has never testified under oath, continues to move forward toward a planned run for the presidency again in 2024.

There can now no longer be any doubt that Trump pressed his false rigged election claim even after he knew he had lost the election. This is established from the unwavering testimony from Trump's own staffers and others presented to the House committee and made public during three hearings thus far. He was so hellbent on being re-elected that even after losing more than 60 lawsuits and hearing from his staff repeatedly that he lost, he continues to this day to repeat his lie that cost five lives on January 6. He simply can't, or won't, handle the truth.

From the House committee, we learned how much pressure Trump applied to Pence to overturn the 2020 election, calling him a "wimp" and provoking an angry mob of supporters that threatened Pence's life.

Retired federal Judge J. Michael Luttig, a Republican conservative who advised Pence ahead of the capital riot, accused Trump and his allies of waging a "war on democracy." He called Trump a "clear and present danger" to American democracy. This is not so much because of what occurred on January 6, but because Trump and his allies have openly and brazenly said they will do whatever they can to assure that either Trump or his handpicked choice wins the 2024 election regardless of the electoral outcome. Indeed, many states have changed their election laws purposely to rig the election outcome if necessary.

"Our democracy today is on a knife's edge," Luttig said.

Patriotism! That word doesn't apply to these scofflaws. Patriots don't violate their code of professional conduct, defy subpoenas, refuse to testify under oath, plead the Fifth Amendment, face jail time, or ask for presidential pardons. And they don't violate the law or oath of office while wrapping themselves in the Constitution.

Although Judge Luttig didn't utter these precise words, his intent is clear: their behavior isn't the stuff of patriotism; it's the stuff of treason.

PREACHING TO THE CHOIR AND OTHER OBSERVATIONS

With President Biden's approval ratings well below 50 percent; with the Democrat Party struggling to find a voice that will resonate with the electorate; with the energy level of the party faithful below that of the extreme right; under normal circumstances, the alternative would be a Republican Party in the mold of Goldwater, Reagan, and Bush which wouldn't be a danger to our basic democratic institutions.

But these are certainly not normal times.

Today's Republican Party is a captive of radical right-wing extremists who are vocal in spewing their bile and hatred masquerading as political opinion, and arrogant enough to say "so what" to those who question them. As we have seen, they've resorted to violence to achieve their goals, and they unabashedly threaten to do it again. To them, January 6 was nothing more than peaceful protestors engaging in legitimate public discourse. This is sheer madness, but it's their reality.

Behind their chief conspirator and bomb-thrower Donald Trump, they have forced the voices of sanity within the party to either retire or face defeat at the polls. They don't care about the nation's historic obedience to the rule of law; they've made up their own.

To them, whatever Trump says is gospel; he can do no wrong. In the eyes of his supporters, he is an innocent victim. What he asks of them is unwavering loyalty to believe exactly what he says, and do exactly what he wants, all in the name of liberty, freedom, and the preservation of our nation. And they give their blind loyalty to him without reservation. He is a charlatan, a fraud, a con artist of the first order. Their reaction: not true or so what! This is a classic example of the cult of personality.

Never mind those annoying facts that get in the way of his rants. Never mind reports documenting his many missteps, failings, and downright lies. His supporters just don't care. Or perhaps they just don't know. Indifference or ignorance. It really doesn't matter.

They're too busy re-writing history and election laws, cutting the legs off the First Amendment and generally engaging in a culture war that undermines the very foundation of our nation.

If their "values" are implicated by others exercising their pesky civil rights and individual liberties founded on our Constitution and laws, the right wing will simply re-interpret the Constitution and re-write the laws.

If they don't like what is being taught in schools, including colleges and universities, they'll just ban those subjects, and install a thought control team to assure what's being taught is righteous and proper according to their standards. And for good measure, they'll create a police-type force to make sure their re-written rule of law is maintained.

Judging from the number of social media posts that see him and his kind for what they really are, there is hope that we can make it through this firestorm with our nation's government, and the Constitution under which it functions, intact.

History is on our side. We overcame a form of extremism during the 1920s and again in the lead-up to World War II. Recall the isolationists who opposed our allies, the Hitler appeasers in Congress and their vocal supporters on the outside, like the America First Committee and its chief spokesman, Charles Lindbergh. It took Pearl Harbor to silence them, but we know all too well that threats to democracy are never permanently silenced. Democracy requires eternal vigilance.

Unfortunately, these social media posts are, to a large extent, tantamount to preaching to the choir. We know there are millions out there who are Trump true believers. How do the voices of sanity reach them, if indeed they are reachable? How do we convince them that real facts matter? That logic matters? That common sense and rationality matter?

Differences of opinion are not what's involved here, and neither are differences of political viewpoints. There is a difference between legitimate political discourse and rank lunacy. Fortunately, most of us know it when we see it.

How do we get through to them that in following a malignant narcissistic authoritarian who has no moral compass and who defines his own rule of law, they are being led toward a cliff, an existential rabbit hole that can only be destructive of what our nation has built over the past 250 years?

Don't they see how many of their fellow loyalists are in jail, or on their way? Do they know that Trump's most vocal allies are resisting every effort at accountability, from ignoring subpoenas, defying Congress, thumbing their collective noses at our judicial system, and on and on? No matter how they try to justify it, attempting to overthrow our government and then denying and defying accountability is not patriotism!

All we have are our voices, and we must remain vocal. This is not the time for uncertainty or timidity. We face a crisis of conscience that is growing, and critical mid-term elections are just around the corner. The threat of electing even more extremists to Congress and other offices of the public trust is real and ominous.

We know what the current Republican Party will do once they regain control of Congress. They have made that abundantly clear. They will impeach Biden because the House dared to impeach Trump for seeking election help from a foreign government in return for congressionally authorized military funding, and for leading an attempted coup based on a lie. The constitutional "high crimes and misdemeanors" standard doesn't matter to them; all they need is a majority vote in the House. Who knows what other draconian punishment methods the right wing will dish out should they gain power? And we know they've threatened more violence in 2024.

While Trump is the main source, he is not the only one who poses such a real threat. He has a number of tinhorn knockoffs; wannabees who, unlike Trump, are true believers in their warped cause of freedom and liberty.

This is where we're headed in the short term. We need our better angels now.

THE CLEAR AND PRESENT DANGER ZONE—REPUBLICAN PROMISES AND A LEADERSHIP VACUUM

The latest poll shows President Biden's approval rating at 39 percent. Going into the November mid-term elections, this is a dangerous sign for the Democrats. So, what are they doing about this?

Perhaps they think the outcome of the House select committee investigating January 6 will turn Biden's disastrous poll numbers around, and by extension help Democrat House and Senate candidates in the fall. Putting all one's eggs in one basket, however, is a risky proposition, especially since it doesn't appear that voter preferences are being altered by the committee's revelations thus far.

Recall that, at his lowest point, Donald Trump polled a 34 percent approval rating. That's two presidencies back-to-back that have polled under 40 percent. I am unable to find any other consecutive presidents who polled less than 40 percent at any time during their respective terms.

There is another poll that shows a majority of Americans believe the country is headed in the wrong direction. What direction is considered the "right" one remains unanswered; however, the poll reveals a general unhappiness and frustration with our government.

There is a clear and present danger here in these poll numbers.

Generally speaking, we are an either-or people. We like two alternatives; any more makes the choice difficult because the public's attention span is, well, let's just say it's limited. This is a compelling reason why third parties have never really taken off electorally. We like to choose between Column A and Column B, between Tweedledee and Tweedledum.

In light of this, if these polls are accurate, then many voters are having great difficulty believing our government truly represents them, as well as finding a national figure who is capable of leading the country in the right direction, whatever that means.

Economic issues usually lie at the heart of voter disappointment and discontent. Gas and food prices, as well as housing and medical costs, are skyrocketing. Income isn't keeping up with rising expenses. When the pocketbook and checkbook are nearing empty, frustration grows. And if the pressure isn't released in a positive way, anger and resentment build to an explosive point. The outcome of such a scenario should be self-evident.

When there is a leadership vacuum—and more and more Americans believe there is—where do they turn for comfort and assurance that all will be fine? There is danger that the wrong kind of person could wind up filling that vacuum.

For a variety of reasons, the voters turned against Trump in 2020. For a variety of reasons, the voters may well turn against Biden this year and take it out on congressional democrats. This is not necessarily because the voters believe they were wrong in 2020; rather the only alternative to the Democrats now in power are the Republicans.

We know what the Republican Party currently stands for, and what its members will do if and when they gain control of Congress after the November elections. The current party leaders have been unabashed in vocalizing their plans. Just yesterday, former president Trump floated the notion of pardoning all those who participated in the January 6 riot at the capital and are now in prison, or face prison. Recall that five lives were lost and over a hundred police officers were injured in that riot.

Ronald Reagan made it very clear when he said "We must reject the idea that every time a law's broken, society is guilty rather than the lawbreaker. It is time to restore the American precept that each individual is accountable for his actions." This applies to Trump, his allies who are enabling him, and those who rioted on his behalf on January 6. It also applies to those who threaten retaliatory action against those who stood up for the Constitution and our democracy during those dark days following the 2020 election, and who to this very day continue to wallow in the lies, deceit and dishonesty that is the current Republican Party.

However, should the Republicans gain control of Congress, and Trump or his handpicked acolyte is successful in 2024, we will be precisely where we were from 2017-2019, with the Republicans in control of both the executive and legislative branches of the federal government. Only this time, they will be far more emboldened to act. And judging from their past conduct and overt arrogance in their promises, those actions could constitute a clear and present danger to our country.

Obviously, by their votes in 2020, a majority of Americans were not satisfied with the Republican party's exercise of power from 2017 to 2019. Taking Republicans at their word, will the voters cast out the Democrats this year and in

2024 in favor of the draconian measures the Republicans promise?

The Republicans lost the White House and the majorities in both houses of Congress in 2020. What is it that tells them that the answer to winning back the White House and Congress are more punitive measures unleashed against those who exercise their individual civil rights and liberties, and against their perceived enemies?

Should the Republicans gain political power again, and should the voters become disenchanted with them, or flatly reject their conduct, there is the real possibility of a vacuum of leadership at the federal level.

This makes clear that there are two sources that give rise to a real national danger zone; Republican promises that are acted upon, and a leadership vacuum.

Where there is global discontent with both political parties, there is resentment. Unresolved or unchecked, it leads to anger. Add anger to a political vacuum where there is no competent leadership, the result is toxic. History is quite clear that what fills that vacuum is a cure that is far worse than the illness.

Be careful out there!

"WHO ARE YOU GONNA BELIEVE, ME OR YOUR LYING EYES?" THE LAW-AND-ORDER HYPOCRISY

According to the latest polls, about 40 percent of Americans believe Trump won the 2020 presidential election. Of that number, 53 percent are Republicans. More than 30 percent of Republicans also believe that the January 6 attack on the nation's capital was "legitimate political discourse."

It's true that some people will believe anything, especially if it's repeated often enough. But these poll numbers translate into tens of millions who reject the 2020 without a single supporting fact. And they believe the "legitimate political discourse" line from the Republican National Committee that can best be explained by the "who are you gonna believe, me or your lying eyes" comedic quote.

Just the other day, the Texas Republican Party approved a measure declaring that President Joe Biden "was not legitimately elected." No facts supporting this, just their belief.

Make no mistake about it; both statements above are lies; all of the evidence proves Trump did not win the presidential election, and the attack on the capital was a conspiracy-driven attempted coup designed to stop the constitutional certification of the election results and keep Trump in power illegally.

History is most revealing about believing lies. As Nazi strongman Joseph Goebbels explained many years ago: "If you tell a lie big enough and keep repeating it, people will eventually come to believe it. The lie can be maintained only for such time as the State can shield the people from the political, economic and/or military consequences of the lie. It thus becomes vitally important for the State to use all of its powers to repress dissent, for the truth is the mortal enemy of the lie, and thus by extension, the truth is the greatest enemy of the State."

Remember Donald Trump's repeated diatribe against the press that dared to criticize him: the press is "truly the enemy of the people." He ratcheted up his use of this derisive label to attack the news media just about every time they pointed out the error of his ways. This is straight out of Goebbels' playbook. Re-read his last sentence: "truth is the mortal enemy of the lie…truth is the greatest enemy of the State." In short, Trump and his allies and supporters, "can't handle the truth."

Remember Trump's "Make America Great Again" slogan? Remember all those red hats? His was not a new slogan. Adolf Hitler used the slogan "Let's make Germany great again," and he was elected leader of Germany. We know how that turned out; we fought a world war over it.

Mark Twain is reputed to have said "A lie can travel halfway around the world before the truth can get its boots on." The incredibly large number of people who believe everything Trump attest to Twain's observation.

Some may treat these two lies as simply statements of political beliefs. Such a notion is bogus and dangerous. Bogus because it's wholly unsupported by any facts and completely devoid of rational thinking. Dangerous because it allows people the comfort of converting any opinion, however draconian or outlandish, to simple political belief, thereby justifying rank lunacy clothed in value judgments.

What we are dealing with here is most assuredly not a mere difference of political beliefs.

The fact that somewhere between 30 million and 50 million Americans believe both Big Lies and support a former president who promises to pardon those January 6 insurrectionists whose crimes led to five deaths and more than 100 injured law enforcement officers, should send chills up our nation's collective spines, or certainly those who believe in facts, who support common sense, who endorse logic and curry rational thinking.

There is nothing rational, logical, factual, or commonsensical about these two categorical lies.

Currently, Republican candidates for public office are trying their best to offer themselves as the law-and-order candidates. Pointedly here in Florida, Sen. Marco Rubio is positioning himself as the champion of law and order over his opponent, Val Demings, a former police officer and chief of the Orlando Police Department. Considering Rubio's silence on Trump's promise to pardon lawbreakers who harmed police officers, his efforts attacking Demings would be laughable. But considering how many millions believe the two Big Lies noted above, he's banking on what Goebbels and Twain said about lying. And as long as it works, officials like Rubio will continue to lie with a straight face.

There is a glaring hypocrisy when it comes to the Republicans' efforts to take the high road on law and order. Typically, their law-and-order cry applies to demonstrations by groups like Antifa, which is their code for blacks, minorities, and their supporters. These demonstrators must be met with aggression in the name of law and order, so they say. If, however, the demonstrators are white, especially white supremacists, then it's not about law and order; it's about love, patriotism, peaceful demonstrators engaging in legitimate political discourse, and on and on. You won't hear the law-and-order reference to demonstrations by right wing extremists because they support the Republican Party, and vocal party members support them. No one is fooled by the party's efforts to corner the law-and-order market. Well, actually, tens of millions are fooled; and so long as they buy whatever the party vocalists sell, they'll continue to sell it.

Truth is the great equalizer, however. Lies must be fought with truth, carefully researched and patiently, but repeatedly and vigorously, expressed. It's the only way out of the swamp we are in.

HOW FAR WILL THE SUPREME COURT GO ON THE SECOND AMENDMENT?

There are many who believe that any restriction on owning and possessing a gun is unconstitutional under the Second Amendment. Under current Supreme Court jurisprudence, they are wrong.

As the leading case of District of Columbia v. Heller (2008), Justice Antonin Scalia, speaking for the Court, said: "Although we do not undertake an exhaustive historical analysis today of the full scope of the Second Amendment, nothing in our opinion should be taken to cast doubt on longstanding prohibitions on the possession of firearms by felons and the mentally ill, or laws forbidding the carrying of firearms in sensitive places such as schools and government buildings, or laws imposing conditions and qualifications on the commercial sale of arms."

Interestingly, so far, courts have excluded concealed carry from constitutional protection, relying on Scalia's observation that "the majority of the 19th-century courts to consider the question held that prohibitions on carrying concealed weapons were lawful under the Second Amendment or state analogues."

Nevertheless, the article below raises deeply held concerns about guns in public and other places where people tend to congregate.

It is recognized that the Constitution means whatever five justices say it says, and the current Court's composition may well upend what Justice Scalia wrote 14 years ago. Since then, we have had far too many mass shootings, and these could well drive Supreme Court action.

Considering the lobbying efforts of the NRA against any gun restrictions, the fact that most Americans want some form of common-sense gun regulations, and a strongly conservative Supreme Court, we will see whether the Second Amendment is interpreted to allow guns, concealed or open carry, in the following places:

The White House
The Supreme Court
Federal courthouses
The nation's capital
State capitols
State courthouses
City halls
Malls and shopping centers
Colleges and universities
Public and private schools
Public and private workplaces

The question that must be asked is whether it makes good sense to allow unrestricted carrying of guns (including the type used in the mass shootings at schools, churches and malls) in the above-listed places, or is the Second Amendment is an absolute, thereby rendering common sense a nullity. Will the Court accept Justice Scalia's admonition, or will the Court depart from his understanding of the amendment? We will see how far the Court and Congress want to go in the name of self-defense.

VIGILANTISM

Republican Parties in deep red states have uniformly condemned those in their respective parties for daring to oppose Donald Trump. Wyoming has roundly condemned Rep. Liz Cheney for challenging Trump's several bogus claims, and for serving as co-chair of the House Select Committee investigating the January 6 attack on the capital. Nebraska and Louisiana are most recently among others who've lashed out at those who dare to question or challenge Trump and Trumpism.

But so far, no other red state comes close to what the Texas Republican Party did just the other day.

Essentially, it takes three elements to create a movement to challenge the status quo: first, identify and crystallize a targeted enemy; second, stir anger and resentment against that enemy by buzzwords that are designed to cause hatred; third, have a gullible audience that is eager to buy into this without question or hesitation.

Texas Republican Sen. Ted Cruz covered all the bases when he addressed the Texas Republican Party. He accused "radical leftists" of driving a cultural assault. Then, he said:

"They want to tear down the church. They want to tear down our schools. They want to tear down our families. They want to tear down our faith. They want to tear down our values."

Notice he didn't describe who the "radical leftists" are. Notice how he hit those things closest to the audience: church, schools, families, faith, values. Notice how he didn't bother explaining how these things are being torn down. Notice that his words contain no facts, no appeal to logic, reason or common sense.

He didn't have to. And it wouldn't serve his purpose.

To his wide-eyed audience gobbling up every word, the enemy is the Democratic Party. The evil the party members are perpetrating is tearing down all those things that the audience values. Cruz certainly served up a heavy portion of red meat to his starving followers.

One report summed up the audience's reaction this way: "attendees said they were fed up. Fed up with elections they believe are rife with fraud. Fed up with their own politicians — including U.S. Sen. John Cornyn, whom they rebuked for taking part in bipartisan talks on gun legislation — for being open to compromise with Democrats. Fed up with the persecution of Christians with traditional values. Fed up with a credulous mainstream media that spouts liberal talking points and disdains anyone who disagrees as racists or bigots. Fed up with undocumented immigrants, even those fleeing war and poverty, for taking advantage of public benefits. Fed up with the education of their children, especially on matters of history and race. Fed up with experts, starting with Dr. Alfred Kinsey, who they said are "sexualizing" students before they've hit puberty."

One pastor said most tellingly: "The enemy is coming in and trying to change our society, change the very fabric of what made America great and they're doing it by going to the children."

Sid Miller, the state agricultural commissioner, said the struggle for America wasn't even partisan anymore.

"The battlefield used to be between Republicans and Democrats. Then it was between conservatives and liberals. Now the battlefield has once again changed. We must improvise, adapt and overcome to defeat our enemy. This new battlefield, this new battlefield is between patriots and traitors."

This, in a nutshell, is what the Republican Party leadership is serving its allies, loyalists and supporters. Resentment, anger, rage—which ultimately leads to action.

And therein lies the existential danger facing our nation.

When a group is sufficiently aroused by pure emotion, focusing anger on a fixed enemy, and the choice they're given is between patriots, which they claim to be, and traitors, which is what the enemy is, then any means necessary to defeat that enemy is justified. In short, to them, violence in the name of patriotism is patriotic.

Notice that Cruz and others never uttered a call for action. They didn't have to. A sufficiently aroused group doesn't need to be told what to do when told the enemy is tearing down everything the group values, and the audience in defending those values are called patriots.

We know what it's called when people take the law into their own hands, serving as arresting officers, prosecutors, judges, juries, and enforcers—all in the name of patriotism and in defense of values, as they define them.

MILLIONS OF GUNS, SEETHING ANGER AND INFLAMMATORY RHETORIC: WHAT COULD POSSIBLY GO WRONG?

It's a sad reality that violence is a significant part of our nation's history. I'm not referring only to the spate of mass shootings and killings in our schools, churches, malls, movie theaters, etc., which are part of our most recent history of violence. I'm also referring to armed conflict.

Whether it's a congressionally declared war, as World Wars I and II were, or a military conflict, like Korea and Vietnam, there is no difference to those whose lives were bleeding out on foreign or domestic soil, or who suffered permanent injuries and disabilities.

To varying degrees, we are familiar with at least some of the wars fought by Americans: the Revolutionary War, the War of 1812, Civil War, Mexican-American War, Spanish-American War, World War I, World War II, Korean War, Vietnam War, Gulf War and the Afghanistan War, just to name a few of the more recognizable ones. Wikipedia lists 102 wars involving America. https://en.wikipedia.org/wiki/List_of_wars_involving_the_United_States

Our nation was founded on violence. The Declaration of Independence of 1776 clearly is a bill of grievances against the king of England. By this declaration, the several colonies threw down the gauntlet to the king with these fighting words:

"....whenever any Form of Government becomes destructive of these ends, it is the Right of the People to alter or to abolish it, and to institute new Government, laying its foundation on such principles and organizing its powers in such form, as to them shall seem most likely to effect their Safety and Happiness."

On August 24, 1814, during the War of 1812, British forces entered Washington, D.C., attacked the Navy Yard, and burned the major federal buildings: the U.S. Capitol, President's House, War Department, and Treasury. It is the only time since the American Revolutionary War that a foreign power had captured and occupied the capital of the United States.

Pointedly, the capital was never subject to a violent attack by a domestic enemy—until January 6, 2021, when the president of the United States whipped up into a frenzy an angry mob of loyal supporters who stormed their way the capital for the express purpose of preventing by force the constitutional transfer of power based on a lie.

There are more than 400 million guns in circulation in America; that exceeds the nation's population by about 40 million. Add to this the amount of seething anger that lies just below the surface, and inflammatory rhetoric by public officials that can ignite the fuse, what could possibly go wrong?

Considering the nation's history of violence, it is not a great leap to envision someone in power knowingly pushing a false grievance designed to whip a crowd into a frenzy and thereby create toxic conditions that ultimately lead to violence. Does this ring a bell?

Recall the oath the president is required by the Constitution to take before assuming office: I do solemnly swear (or affirm) that I will faithfully execute the Office of President of the United States, and will to the best of my ability, preserve, protect and defend the Constitution of the United States."

President Donald Trump, in unleashing the mob assault on the capital, did not "preserve, protect and defend the Constitution of the United States."

Note the oath taken by members of Congress before they are permitted to assume office: "I do solemnly swear (or affirm) that I will support and defend the Constitution of the United States against all enemies, foreign and domestic; that I will bear true faith and allegiance to the same; that I take this obligation freely, without any mental reservation or purpose of evasion; and that I will well and faithfully discharge the duties of the office on which I am about to enter: So help me God."

Those members of Congress who aided and abetted in any way the January 6 insurrection and attempted coup, and to this day avoid accountability, did not "support and defend the Constitution of the United States against all enemies, foreign and domestic."

In a complete reversal of reality, those who attacked the capital are hailed as patriots by these officials hellbent on pushing a false narrative, while those who stood up for the Constitution and rule of law are branded as traitors.

We have public officials openly calling for rebellion by telling their unyielding supporters to "take back" their government, as if their government has been taken away from them.

These officials are violating their oaths by declaring that the "enemy" (meaning the Democrats) is taking away their churches, schools, etc. This of course is both bogus and nonsense. No one is taking away anything from these people. But it's not about rationality; it's about anger, hatred and belief.

The specter of these public officials stoking violence, turning Americans against Americans, is contrary to everything our nation stands for.

What this type of rhetoric does is to justify violence as patriotic; it also justifies those who hold particular religious beliefs from preventing others with different beliefs from freely exercising them. When one religion is given supremacy over the doctrines and belief systems of others, the seeds of violence are planted, the consequences self-evident.

Yet, this is what those who swore allegiance to our Constitution are doing, and they're doing this right in front of our eyes, daring the rest to do something about it.

Our better angels must not let this form of tyranny stand. We are in dangerous times; sane officials and pundits make this clear every day. We must do everything in our power to make the rule of law mean precisely that. We must be governed by facts, not rage; by common sense, not violence; by truth, not lies. If not stopped, we will suffer the pain of violence again. And again.

WHAT ARE THE REAL CONSERVATIVE VALUES?

It's that time of year when political campaigning moves into high gear. And with every Republican candidate passing himself/herself off as a promoter of "conservative values" or "Christian conservative values," it's important to know precisely what they mean when they wrap themselves in this self-righteous cloak.

We're certainly familiar with the usual conservative refrain: Individual Freedom. Limited Government. The Rule of Law. Peace through Strength. Fiscal Responsibility. Free Markets. Human Dignity. But what are these conservative values in actual practice?

Let's begin with the case of Eric Greitens, the former governor of Missouri who's running for the United States Senate. Greitens was elected governor of Missouri in 2016, but he resigned less than two years later amid allegations of sexually assaulting and blackmailing a woman with whom he had an extramarital affair.

His recent campaign ad prompted accusations of glorifying political violence. "Today, we're going RINO hunting," Greitens said with a smile as he slid the action on his shotgun in the 38-second ad. RINO stands for "Republican in name only." Greitens and a team of men outfitted in military gear are then shown bursting into a home, guns raised. "The RINO feeds on corruption and is marked by the stripes of cowardice," said Greitens. "Get a RINO hunting permit. There's no bagging limit, no tagging limit, and it doesn't expire until we save our country." This is an unbridled appeal to violence. He seems to be doing well in the polls.

Is he an example of conservative values?

Georgia Rep. Majorie Taylor Greene repeatedly indicated support for political violence and execution of top Democrats and FBI agents. She has promoted violent, deranged conspiracy theories online; peddled conspiracies that mass shootings were false flags and "staged;" and spread anti-Muslim and anti-Semitic comments and conspiracies.

Is she an example of conservative values?

Next up is Arizona Rep. Paul Gosar. While the sane among us were mourning the massacre of school children and their teachers, Rep. Gosar was pandering to his supporters, using the shooter to advance the far right's culture wars.

Gosar announced to the world that the alleged shooter, 18-year-old Salvador Ramos, was "a transsexual leftist illegal alien." Of course, there isn't a single fact that supported his nonsense. You might recall he was censured for posting a video showing himself killing a congresswoman and threatening the president. Not a single Republican leader in his state denounced him, and he'll most likely be re-elected in a landslide.

Is he an example of conservative values?

(For some Republicans, Greene's and Gosar's behavior was just too much to stomach. Both were criticized for speaking at a white nationalist gathering. But what about their constituents? Will they vote to remove these two who, by their words and deeds, have demonstrated their unfitness for public office? Again, do these two public officials represent conservative values?)

Just the other day, we learned that Wisconsin Sen. Ron Johnson tried to transmit Wisconsin's fake electoral votes to congress in an effort to overturn the results of the 2020 presidential election. He did this after more than 60 court decisions debunked Donald Trump's Big Lie "rigged election" claim. Facts didn't stop him; loyalty to one man trumped his loyalty to his oath of office.

Does he represent conservative values?

Then there are the 147 Republicans who, with no factual predicate and for the sole purpose of appeasing Donald Trump and endorsing his Big Lie, voted to overturn the presidential election results and thwart the constitutional process for the orderly transfer of power.

Is this what Republicans mean by conservative values?

The Texas Republicans Party is on record as declaring Joe Biden illegitimately elected even though every court considering this ludicrous claim rejected it.

Is this demonstrative of conservative values?

And then there's the Big Liar himself, still forging ahead with, in the words of his former Attorney General Bill Barr, BS that plays well to his base, but no one else.

Is Donald Trump the ultimate exemplar of conservative values? And does the base represent conservative values?

Then there's the House select committee hearings on January 6. Republican state officials testified how they steadfastly refused to go along with the unconstitutional actions by Trump and his allies.

So, which side represents true conservative values, Trump and his loyalists who sought to pervert their oaths and the Constitution, or those Republican officials who stood by their oaths and the Constitution?

Let's look at two of the conservatives' favorite pitching points, individual freedom and the rule of law.

Try the individual freedom line on a woman who wants an abortion. How about a teacher who wants to teach the history of the civil rights movement—not the sanitized version, but the real history? How about a business owner who is critical of a republican official's stand on a particular issue, and faces statutorily sanctioned punishment for daring to speak out? How about those republican governors and legislators who passed laws allowing citizens to sue citizens because of hurt feelings? What about their individual freedom to speak as guaranteed by the First Amendment?

Is this what conservatives mean about individual freedom?

And for rule of law, tell that to the five who died during the January 6 attack on the capital, or the more than 140 law enforcement officers who were injured while protecting the capital from an angry, unruly mob of Trump supporters. Or tell that to the law enforcement officers in Idaho who have received death threats for arresting white supremacists near a gay pride event. These scofflaws are called patriots by far-right politicians.

Are these examples of what conservatives mean by the rule of law? Or what they mean about human dignity? Are those who foment and carry out acts of violence under the false flag of patriotism exemplars of conservative values?

There are many other examples of situations where the conduct doesn't match the words, but you get the idea.

Taking all of this into account, it is a legitimate question to ask what precisely conservatives mean when they wrap themselves around "conservative values?" Do the actions taken by Republicans like those referenced above represent conservative values, or are conservative values represented by the so-called RINOs Greitens and his ilk complain about?

Actions do speak louder than words.

INDOCTRINATION, RELIGION AND REALITY

When Florida Republican Governor Ron DeSantis signed legislation giving families and children, businesses and employees, authority to fight discrimination and woke indoctrination, he said: In Florida, we will not let the far-left woke agenda take over our schools and workplaces. There is no place for indoctrination or discrimination in Florida." This legislation is the first of its kind in the nation to take on both corporate wokeness and Critical Race Theory in schools in onc act.

Read DeSantis' quote again. Focus on the words "There is no place for indoctrination…in Florida." I guess DeSantis doesn't attend church very often.

What precisely does he think takes place in houses of worship? Religion is defined as "the process of teaching a person or group to accept a set of beliefs uncritically." Indoctrination is "the process of teaching a person or group to accept a set of beliefs uncritically." Both definitions require uncritical acceptance of a set of beliefs. That's indoctrination.

In just about every academic discipline, we are taught to think critically. Critical thinking is "the intellectually disciplined process of actively and skillfully conceptualizing, applying, analyzing, synthesizing, and/or evaluating information gathered from, or generated by, observation, experience, reflection, reasoning, or communication, as a guide to belief and action." Our jobs might well require this. We use these analytical skills in dealing with advertisements, so we're not ripped off. We avoid scams by thinking through what others are trying to sell us. And on and on.

This is not the case with religion. Religious beliefs are just that, beliefs. Members of a religious group are asked to accept the religion's dogma or doctrine; that is "the written body of teachings of a religious group that are generally accepted by that group." The doctrine, creed, or gospel is accepted wholeheartedly and without reservation as an article of faith. Critical thinking and religious beliefs do not go hand in hand. They are not meant to.

I've been in the Vatican, Westminster Abbey in London, Notre Dame Cathedral in Paris and Montreal, Hagia Sophia and the Blue Mosque in Istanbul, the Church of the Savior of the Spilled Blood in St. Petersburg, Russia, among others. The enormity of these houses of worship, and their ecclesiastical interiors, are sights to behold and attest to the enormous power and value of faith.

Religion is an overwhelmingly powerful force. A belief system gives believers a sense of purpose, a reason for being, and value to life now and in the afterlife. Yet, how many were told something like this when growing up and learning to ask questions, specifically about religion: "God's ways are not for us to understand, they are for us to believe in, you just need to have more faith."

It has been said that critical thinking is anathema to religious doctrine. Psychological studies note that religious individuals are less likely to engage logical processes and be less efficient at detecting reasoning conflicts; therefore, they are more likely to take intuitive answers at face value. Logic and rational thought take a back seat when people are asked to accept religious dogma.

What happens when the mindset necessary for ready acceptance of religious doctrine is transferred to other disciplines, like politics? When political leaders ask for ready acceptance of their word, what are the faithful to do? Assuming the faithful are also required to use critical thinking and its analytical tools in their everyday lives, when they are asked to suspend them for religious instruction and for certain types of political speeches, what are the faithful to do?

I think we see this in the religious fervor surrounding Donald Trump, Trumpism and right-wing zealotry. Blind acceptance of his word. Denial of any facts or evidence that is contradictory to his word. Beliefs are not and cannot be questioned. For the deeply religious person, when belief is challenged by fact, belief prevails. No one in a country governed by Sharia Law dares question it.

Religion is indeed a vital force and has an essential role in an ordered society. But when religion trumps the secular; when it permeates attitudes, activities, or other things that have no religious or spiritual basis; specifically, when religion becomes an ultimate driving force politically, then the result is a theocracy. I don't think there's an American who wants our country to be compared with the theocratic countries like Afghanistan, Iran, Sudan, Saudi Arabia, Yemen, etc. History teaches what life is like in church run governments. We must not take that path. This is precisely why our forefathers erected a wall between church and state—a wall that is crumbling because of the conservative wing of the Supreme Court.

Meanwhile, Gov. DeSantis and other far-right Republicans are cleverly using religious buzzwords to accuse others of the misdeeds that they themselves are doing. Their latest effort is the word "indoctrination." While DeSantis and others rail against far-left indoctrination, they have no problem with far-right indoctrination. We know DeSantis covets this.

As one reporter notes, "DeSantis claims that just about everyone but his political allies are trying to indoctrinate children into questionable beliefs, including college professors, public school teachers and companies such as Disney. But the reality is that Florida Republicans are seeking to force schools and businesses to promote their political agenda.

The GOP-controlled Legislature has passed, and DeSantis has signed into law, measures aimed at stopping schools and businesses from offering classes, books or worker training sessions that teach tolerance toward others or an understanding of racism and other discrimination in our country. At the same time, schools are being forced to install a curriculum focused on teaching the evils of socialism, the blessings of liberty and the infallibility of the Founding Fathers."

Of course, the true believers won't accept any of this as true, just like they won't accept anything negative about Trump, his allies and loyalists. Why?

Because they are indoctrinated not to.

AH, THE SECOND AMENDMENT!

The United States Supreme Court has now declared that the Second Amendment allows people to carry concealed weapons outside the home for the purpose of self-defense. More accurately, the six-member conservative bloc on the Court made this declaration.

The decision allows states to prohibit guns in "sensitive places," likely applying to locations such as courthouses and legislative buildings and others that historically meet that definition. These places usually have a police presence, and that may become a significant factor in future cases. As a dissenting justice asked: "So where does that leave the many locations in a modern city with no obvious 18th- or 19th-century analogue? What about subways, nightclubs, movie theaters and sports stadiums? The court does not say."

Presumably, this "sensitive places" question will be asked in future cases as this term applies to those locations where people congregate but may or may not have a police presence. And by this, I don't mean mall cops armed only with a walkie-talkie. It should be quite evident that an officer armed only with a walkie-talkie, or a baton, will not prevent an attack by someone hellbent on carrying out mass murder with an assault-type weapon.

Tom King, president of the New York State Rifle and Pistol Association, the NRA's state affiliate, said he would like to see as few places deemed "sensitive" as possible, and would file legal challenges if, for example, officials tried to ban weapons on subways or buses. There is no general police presence on either a bus or in the subway. In any event, leave it to the NRA to launch further litigation against any laws that are designed to protect public safety.

Fortunately, the Court did not bar states from imposing requirements on people seeking licenses to carry firearms including fingerprinting, background checks, mental health checks and firearms training classes.

Nothing in this decision considers how to prevent the epidemic of mass shootings we have witnessed over the past several years. What is to prevent the self-defender from becoming an assaulter, attacking a church, school, mall, etc.? The answer: nothing.

We know there will be more mass shootings; every statistic tells us this. But after the next one, how will the right wing respond? If history is any guide, we'll hear "It's not the gun, it's mental illness." We'll hear that it's not the gun owner, it's the criminals who shouldn't have guns. And we'll hear the tired, hackneyed "thoughts and prayers." More and more families of victims of mass shootings are telling those "thoughts and prayers" officials where they can stick their feigned sympathy.

As for the "mental health" comfort zone, I doubt sane, intelligent, compassionate people suddenly decide to commit mass murder with an assault rifle. But mental health usually doesn't enter the picture until it's too late; after the crime has been committed. Blaming "mental health" for these horrific crimes is a strawman because it solves nothing, while giving a bogus defense to those who simply won't face the fact that a nut with a gun is far more deadly than a nut who can't access a weapon. And too often we don't know who the nut is until it's too late.

As for the "criminals" defense, it is a fact that these shooters aren't criminals until after they engage in mass murder with an assault rifle. How do you stop them before they become "criminals?" You can't. Taking this into account, saying it's all about criminals is nonsense.

On the matter of self-defense, the facts show this claim to be disingenuous. Statistics show that people use guns for self-defense only rarely. According to a Harvard University analysis of figures from the National Crime Victimization Survey, people defended themselves with a gun in nearly

0.9 percent of crimes from 2007 to 2011. That's less than one percent! Self-defense is the battle cry; it's the rationale behind the Court's decision. The facts simply don't support it.

David Hemenway, who led the Harvard research, argues that the risks of owning a gun outweigh the benefits of having one in the rare case where you might need to defend yourself. "The average person ... has basically no chance in their lifetime ever to use a gun in self-defense. But ... every day, they have a chance to use the gun inappropriately. They have a chance, they get angry. They get scared."

Finally, on a related matter of gun violence, the House select committee investigating that attempted coup on January 6, 2021, revealed for the first time that several Republican members of Congress sought a pardon from Donald Trump for their efforts in pressing his lies about a rigged election and giving aid and comfort to the rioters. This means these scofflaws knew they were lying to their constituents for the express purpose of riling them up in support of Trump.

What does this say about how these public officials really feel about the intelligence of their constituents?

AFTER THE HOUSE JANUARY 6 COMMITTEE HEARINGS, WHAT'S NEXT?

After five committee hearings dissecting the January 6 attack on the nation's capital in an attempted coup by supporters of Donald Trump, it should be obvious that criminal charges and prosecution loom on the horizon.

Charges could be filed against Trump, as well as some of his staunch allies. It's not difficult to figure out who else might be charged. Just note those who defied congressional subpoenas and await trial for contempt of Congress. (Steve Bannon, Mark Meadows and Peter Navarro)

Then, add those members of Congress who asked Trump for a pardon. (The list is made up of Trump's closest congressional allies: Republican Reps. Mo Brooks of Alabama, Matt Gaetz of Florida, Andy Biggs of Arizona, Louie Gohmert of Texas, Scott Perry of Pennsylvania and Marjorie Taylor Greene of Georgia.) They wouldn't have done that if they didn't believe they committed a crime.

Then add the remaining 141 Republicans who voted to overturn the election results of 2020, including those who adamantly told the committee they wouldn't testify under any circumstance.

Of course, if any in these last two groups are indicted, they will predictably claim that "it's a witch hunt," or "a hatchet job" or a "partisan hit job," etc. Never mind that just about all of the televised testimony is from Republicans, including those who worked for Trump. And never mind they testified under oath; something that neither Trump nor his recalcitrant loyalists have done yet.

What actual crimes could be filed against Trump? It appears there are four major areas the congressional committee's is focusing on: 1. Obstruction of an official proceeding of Congress 2. Conspiracy to defraud the United States 3. Seditious conspiracy 4. Wire fraud. Wrapped in these four charges is a host of campaign finance laws he could be charged with violating both before and during his term. And there are potential state criminal law charges he could face in Georgia for election tampering and related crimes, and in New York. There may be others out there as well that are currently below the radar screen.

The filing of criminal charges, however, is just the first step in the criminal justice system. Once charges are filed, a defendant is entitled to the presumption of innocence. The government must prove its case by the highest of evidentiary burdens: beyond and to the exclusion of any reasonable doubt. And remember that no defendant is found guilty unless and until a jury of his peers determines guilt.

Selecting a jury will be dicey at best. With so many MAGA loyalists out there, those who are fact-deniers, reality deniers, conspiracy theorists, etc., who believe Trump is the victim of a vast conspiracy, among other off-the-wall things, getting a jury to convict under our criminal justice standards will not be easy. For potential jurors like these, questions about belief will be important.

In the selection of a jury, lawyers on both sides are entitled to question prospective jurors. This is called voir dire, and its purpose is to make as certain as possible that the jury is composed of fair-minded, competent people who can pass judgment based on the facts as presented in court, and the law as instructed by the judge.

Considering the MAGA influence, voir dire will have to be carefully tailored. Since right wing supporters are fed the line of individual responsibility and personal accountability, questions will have to be directed to those core values. It's entirely possible that the prosecution lawyers will ask such questions as "Do you believe that everyone is personally accountable for their behavior?" "Do you believe Donald Trump is accountable and responsible for his own behavior?" "Do you believe Donald Trump is capable of committing crimes?" "If the facts show that Donald Trump committed crimes, will you be able to find him guilty?" Etc., etc., etc.

Of course, the judge has a say over the extent of these types of questions, and a judge who happens to be a Trump appointee and supporter might have a different take than one who isn't.

But all of this is speculation at this time, and there is much more that must take place before we reach this post-committee point.

There are more hearings scheduled; more Republican witnesses to lay out Trump's actions, and those of his allies. Nothing the committee presents will cast Trump and his sycophants in a favorable light.

And then there's the committee's final report. I doubt this committee will make the same mistake as the Special Counsel Robert Mueller investigation into Russian interference in the 2016 United States elections, links between associates of Donald Trump and Russian officials, and possible obstruction of justice by Trump and his associates: issue a lengthy, tepid report with vague conclusions.

So, it's only going to get worse for Trump. Ultimately, however, it will be up to our criminal justice system to decide what to do with Donald Trump. (And the voters, should he decide to run again. But that's another story.) To be sure, our system is imperfect, but it is still the best the world has ever seen.

ENERGIZING THE BASE—BY THE DEMOCRATS

The Democrat Party has been on the receiving end of harsh criticism from its own supporters for being wishy-washy in dealing with the right wing's wild and wholly ways, particularly over the past six years. Party faithful have been frustrated by weak, feckless responses—and even silence—in the face of the right wing's explosive rhetoric and daring threatened actions.

The Supreme Court's ruling overturning abortion rights under Roe v. Wade provides the opportunity to tamp down that criticism and energize the party's base, and beyond. Polls show that a majority of Americans favor a woman's right to choose. (Further, polls also show a majority favor more restrictive gun regulation, such as getting assault rifles off the streets.)

Make no mistake about it: this overruling of the nearly 50-year constitutional right to choose is a religion-driven decision favored by a minority of Americans. Similarly, opposition to common sense gun regulations has a minority religious foundation.

Wheaton College's Institute for the Study of American Evangelicals estimates that about 30 to 35 percent (90 to 100 million people) of the U.S. population is evangelical. These figures include white and black "cultural evangelicals" (Americans who do not regularly attend church but identify as evangelicals).

Approximately 74% percent of White Evangelicals oppose abortion, and white evangelical Protestants are some of the strongest supporters of gun rights who oppose further restrictions.

The only way to protect a woman's right to choose, and to enact further reasonable gun regulations, is to change the composition of Congress and several state legislatures and governors.

The passage of current gun regulation legislation will tamp down somewhat the demand for more restrictive legislation directed to easy access, but considering the NRA's stance against any further "sensitive places" restrictions, deep concerns by a majority of the voters remain on the table.

And any future mass shootings will only further anger these voters who will demand more regulations.

There is a third element that is also religion-driven: the rise of Donald Trump and Trumpism. In 2016, Trump received 81% of the Evangelical Christian vote; in 2020, that number was 75%. Pointedly, Trump never received a majority popular vote; it was the Electoral College that carried Trump to victory in 2016.

Going into the November elections, the voters will have before them three boiling issues: abortion rights, gun regulations and from the televised House committee hearings and what will most assuredly be a devastating final report, a corrupt Trump presidency.

Both parties will be framing their campaigns around these three blockbusters. For drastically different reasons, neither will be able to avoid this. The democrats will use these issues like a weapon; the republicans will have to justify their anti-abortion, pro-gun, pro-Trump stance. The debate will be over who can best arouse their base and motivate them to vote. Clearly, the republicans have the advantage of an already aroused base. It will also be interesting to see how the parties attempt to draw independents into their respective folds.

The Republicans have been extremely successful in hammering away at "liberal leftists" who favor a "socialist agenda," while standing for "freedom, liberty and the rule of law." Great sound bites.

The Democrats have thus far failed in their efforts to hammer away at the Republicans for claimed draconian actions that don't match their sound bites and buzzwords.

There are collateral hot-button issues that arise from this latest abortion decision. Over the years, the Supreme Court has ruled that the rights to "personal autonomy, bodily integrity, self-dignity, and self-determination" are protected by the Due Process Clause. This is called substantive due process. Together, these interests are invoked to justify a constitutionally protected right to privacy.

This issue was first addressed in 1965 when the Supreme Court ruled that it was unconstitutional for a state law to prohibit married adults from using contraception. Other rights that the Supreme Court has declared are protected by the right to privacy include: the right for parents to raise their children as they see fit, the right for extended family members to share a home, the right for competent adults to refuse life-saving medical procedures, and the right to engage in same-sex sexual relations, including same-sex marriage.

Justice Clarence Thomas, in his concurring opinion, said abortion is not enough; he wants the Court to consider birth control and same sex marriage decisions that are premised on substantive due process privacy rights. In fact, Thomas could well put into play all rights derived from "the right to be let alone" which lies at the heart of the right to privacy.

But with this latest decision from the Supreme Court, coupled with their rigid stand in favor of guns via open carry and "constitutional carry," and a former president and his loyalists wallowing in disgrace, the Republican Party has handed the Democrat Party three issues of varying but great intensity. All of these issues with be on the ballot in November.

Justice Thomas assures there will undoubtedly be others; perhaps he will lobby the Court for a thorough re-examination of the civil rights jurisprudence beginning with Brown v. Board of Education almost 70 years ago. The fact is we don't know what the reach of the Court's conservative majority might well portend down the road.

Taking all of these matters into consideration, this represents the democrats' best opportunity. If the party is to remain viable, it had better seize it.

WAKING THE SLEEPING GIANT

From the sheer volume of social media postings roundly condemning the United States Supreme Court's conservative majority for overruling the constitutional right to an abortion, and the protests held nationwide, I am reminded of what was said after Japan bombed Pearl Harbor on December 7, 1941.

Following President Franklin Roosevelt's speech to Congress the following day in which he said a state of war existed between us and Japan, Japanese Admiral Isoroku Yamamoto, who planned the attack on Pearl Harbor, would reportedly write in his diary, "I fear all we have done is to awaken a sleeping giant and fill him with a terrible resolve."

Japan did indeed awaken a sleeping giant, filling our country with a "terrible resolve," and the Land of the Rising Sun paid dearly for its unpremeditated attack less than four years later in August 1945, when Hiroshima and Nagasaki were decimated by the power of the atomic bomb.

Flash forward to today.

In the most recent poll conducted by Pew Research, a 61% majority of U.S. adults say abortion should be legal in all or most cases. Among Republicans and Republican-leaning independents, 60% of moderates and liberals say abortion should be legal in all or most cases, compared with just 27% of conservative Republicans.

The bottom line is that a significant majority of American voters favor the legalization of abortion. The Supreme Court is woefully out of step with the national consensus here.

That is the sleeping giant that the abortion decision may well have awakened. We will certainly find out in November.

Considering the number of states that enacted draconian restrictions on registration and voting following the 2020 presidential election in support of Donald Trump's Big Lie, efforts to get that giant in the form of tens of millions of voters to cast their votes will be daunting.

There must be no doubt that it will take a herculean effort mobilize voters to get out the vote. And the effort must be continuous, concerted and not limited solely to democrats. There is no doubt the Court's decision on abortion, and the threat to re-visit other constitutional privacy rights like access to contraceptives, same sex marriage and same sex sexual relations, is driven by the 27% rigidly conservative Republican minority. It is this group that is waging the culture war against civil rights and civil liberties. All in the name of freedom, of course.

The voting public needs to be reminded from this day going forward just exactly how the extreme religious right has commandeered the Republican Party. The party officeholders beholden to this group need to know that they were elected by a vocal minority.

A concerted campaign on these hot-button issues, and a vigorous get-out-the-vote plan, all directed to the awakened giant, is the only way out of this morass. If it is necessary to end the filibuster, then so be it.

Once this great majority of voters decide they will no longer stand by and watch years of blood, toil, sweat and tears expended in forging civil rights and civil liberties simply washed away by the right wing, they will "take back our country." And all the obstacles the far right placed in voting won't stop them.

REPUBLICANS ARE REACTIONARIES

Republicans on the far right accuse democrats of being "progressive," using this word in connection with their old standby, "socialism." This, they believe, allows them use "progressive" as an epithet, something to be soundly rejected by their gullible, unsophisticated audience.

Apparently, they haven't seen fit to look up the definition of "progressive." Here it is: In current politics, progressivism is "a social or political movement that aims to represent the interests of ordinary people through political change and the support of government actions."

While accusing democrats of being progressive, they wrap themselves around, and proudly wear the badge of, anti-Wokeness. Again, apparently, they haven't seen fit to look up the word "woke." Woke means being "aware of and actively attentive to important facts and issues (especially issues of racial and social justice)." That's it.

Therefore, what anti-woke Republicans are really saying is that they are unaware of these important issues and are proud of their ignorance or indifference to them.

From the definitions above, progressives seek to represent the interests of "ordinary people" and therefore are aware of and actively attentive to important facts and issues, especially pertaining to race and social justice. Far-right republicans on the other hand are happy in their ignorance or indifference, wearing this as a badge of honor.

This means these republicans are reactionaries. In popular usage, "reactionary refers to a strong traditionalist conservative political perspective of the person who is opposed to social, political, and economic change. Reactionary ideologies can be radical in the sense of political extremism in service to re-establishing past conditions."

History shows the harmful effects reactionaries have had on our nation. The reactionaries were in vogue during the post-World War I period; their reign ended temporarily when their policies led to the stock market crash in 1929. They held the upper hand in Congress as Hitler gained more and more power in the 1930s. Their chief spokesman, Charles Lindbergh, argued vociferously for appeasing Hitler. We know how that worked out. It took Pearl Harbor to shove the reactionaries to the side during World War II. Of course, they never really went away.

Historian Heather Cox Richardson capsulized them in one of her recent articles this way:

"The current-day Republican Party has abandoned the idea of a democracy in which a majority of the people elect their government. Instead, its members have embraced minority rule."

Overturning Roe v. Wade "marks the end of an era: the period in American history stretching from 1933 to 1981, the era in which the U.S. government worked to promote democracy. It tried to level the economic playing field between the rich and the poor by regulating business and working conditions. It provided a basic social safety net through programs like Social Security and Medicare and, later, through food and housing security programs. It promoted infrastructure like electricity and highways, and clean air and water, to try to maintain a basic standard of living for Americans. And it protected civil rights by using the Fourteenth Amendment, added to the U.S. Constitution in 1868, to stop states from denying their citizens the equal protection of the laws.

Now the Republicans are engaged in the process of dismantling that government. For forty years, the current Republican Party has worked to slash business regulations and the taxes that support social welfare programs, to privatize infrastructure projects, and to end the federal protection of civil rights by arguing for judicial "originalism" that claims to honor the original version of the Constitution rather than permitting the courts to protect rights through the Fourteenth Amendment.

But most Americans actually like the government to hold the economic and social playing field level. So, to win elections, Republicans since 1986 have suppressed votes, flooded the media with propaganda attacking those who like government action as dangerous socialists, gerrymandered congressional districts, abused the Senate filibuster to stop all Democratic legislation, and finally, when repeated losses in the popular vote made it clear their extremist ideology would never again command a majority, stacked the Supreme Court.

The focus of the originalists on the court has been to slash the federal government and make the states, once again, the centerpiece of our democratic system. That democracy belonged to the states was the argument of the southern Democrats before the Civil War, who insisted that the federal government could not legitimately intervene in state affairs. At the same time, though, state lawmakers limited the vote in their state, so "democracy" did not reflect the will of the majority. It reflected the interests of those few who could vote.

State governments, then, tended to protect the power of a few wealthy, white men, and to write laws reinforcing that power. Southern lawmakers defended human enslavement, for example, a system that concentrated wealth among a few white men. Challenged to defend their enslavement of their neighbors in a country that boasted "all men are created equal," they argued that enslavement was secondary to the fact that voters had chosen to impose it."

This is where the reactionaries want to take the nation. Back to a darker, more sinister time in our history. Enlightenment is not part of their vocabulary.

It's time for the waking giant to take the upper hand.

WHY DO CONSERVATIVE SUPREME COURT JUSTICES FAVOR ORIGINALISM?

Conservative justices on the Supreme Court pride themselves on being originalists; that is, those who interpret the Constitution according to the text and intent of the framers. They confidently say that other justices who interpret the nation's founding charter according to contemporary times are simply wrong and misguided.

To these conservative justices, the Constitution is "dead," echoing the word of the late guru of originalism, Justice Antonin Scalia.

Originalism is, of course, one theory of constitutional interpretation; the other is called "living constitutionalism," allowing for interpretation designed to meet current or contemporary conditions or standards. The constitution itself provides no means for correctly interpreting it; that's left to the judiciary.

Given the recent rulings by the six-member conservative majority on the Court, most notably its decision to overturn a constitutional right for the first time in our nation's history in rejecting Roe v. Wade, the logical question arises: why do conservatives favor treating the Constitution as a dead document? Why originalism?

The answer is obvious.

When the Constitution was ratified in 1788, our nation's population was just under 4 million, spread across 13 states and territories. The largest city was Philadelphia, with just over 40,000 population. There was no interstate rail system. No interstate highway system. No airplanes. No trains. No cars. No skyscrapers. No inner cities. No real infrastructure. Medicine and science were archaic. It was the horse-and-buggy days. Life generally involved working the land in the largely rural United States.

The nation has grown exponentially since then. Now, a population of 4 million could easily be found in any of our nation's largest cities—and the population of each of those cities actually exceeds 4 million.

Today, we are a nation of 50 states stretching thousands of miles from sea to sea and border to border, with two states far beyond. Our vast expanse of occupied land has a population of about 340 million and growing. Our nation has interstate rail, air and highway systems spread throughout. We have technology that is wholly alien to our founding fathers. The same can be said about science and medicine. Advances in technology, science and medicine are continuing at a geometric pace. Urban areas will continue to expand. We have large colleges and universities that didn't exist back then. Meanwhile, rural areas continue to shrink.

Despite the overwhelmingly explosive growth of our nation over the past 234 years, we have justices who are all-too-willing to apply the Constitution written for 4 million living in largely rural America, to the needs and interests of a dynamic and diverse population of 340 million.

Back then, there was no need to address how 340 million people lived worked, raised a family, retired, etc., under one national umbrella, literally side by side. Social services, civil and human rights really didn't matter in the grand scheme of things; putting food on the table, tending to the farm, etc., were far more important.

There are two other factors that must be considered in asking this question of conservative justices. First, conservatives favor business over individuals. There is no better example than during the 1930s when conservative justices rejected much of Franklin Roosevelt's New Deal legislation designed to deal with the Great Depression—brought about largely as a result of the economic policies of Presidents Harding, Coolidge and Hoover. Remember Calvin Coolidge's "The business of America is business."

Second, conservative justices trend strongly toward the religious right. The Court's abortion and gun regulations decisions roundly attest to that.

Taking these two matters into account, it's easy to see why conservative justices favor the horse-and-buggy approach toward the Constitution. It makes it easy for them to reject out of hand any legislation that might adversely impact either business or the religious right. If civil rights, hot-button human rights, or a vast network of social services didn't exist back then, they surely can't find a basis in the

Constitution under the originalism approach. And these programs cost money, and that money must, to varying degrees, come from businesses either out-of-pocket or through taxes. Tax breaks for businesses are beneficial, but beside the point here. Originalism provides a convenient way to reject moderate-to-liberal social programs, among other things.

Opposing the "living Constitution" approach, conservative justices say any changes in the law to reflect current conditions is a matter for the Congress. However, the specter of asking politicians dependent on campaign finances to decide what civil, social, and other personal rights should be given to the public is anathema to our nation's heritage since the 1930s. Unlike laws, which are forged through compromise and negotiation—trade-offs–rights shouldn't be so fashioned. The Constitution is foundational, and the Supreme Court is the final arbiter of what the Constitution means. By way of example, nowhere in the Constitution do the words "Miranda warning" appear, yet the Supreme Court has declared such warning necessary to assure the constitutionally guaranteed right to a fair trial. In short, there are times when the legislative process simply doesn't work to protect what the Constitution guarantees. Due process, equal protection, privileges and immunities are among the undefined phrases in the Constitution. Only the Supreme Court can give life ultimate life to them, not the Congress.

As a backup argument, originalists say that changed conditions can be addressed by constitutional amendment process. A quick review of the history of constitutional amendments exposes the folly of such a claim.

There have been 27 amendments since the Constitution's ratification. That's 27 over a 234-year period. The first 10 were adopted in 1791; meaning only 17 were adopted over the past 230 years. Since 1920, only 9 amendments have been adopted, none since 1992. A dynamic society needs a Constitution that keeps up with the times, not one that is steeped in the past and can only move forward at the speed of a glacier.

Living constitutionalists know they must apply the Constitution to a far more complex world than that of our forefathers. They are cognizant of current societal conditions and what is needed to keep up with them. They know about the rapid shifts that can occur in a dynamic, mobile society. They know the law must not be stifled by judicial lag.

Originalists want nothing to do with that. Protecting business, the wealthy and the interests of the religious right fit comfortably in the originalist approach.

If these conservative justices were given a choice of riding to work in a horse and buggy, or in a Lexis or Acura, we all know which one they would choose. Would they want to be treated with 18th century medicine? Drive on 18th century roads? You get the picture.

So why would they apply a horse-and-buggy Constitution to deal with today's dynamic, fluid society? Asked and answered.

Printed in the United States
by Baker & Taylor Publisher Services